**Bedtime
Sucks**

Bedtime Sucks

What to Do When You and Your Baby Are Cranky, Sleep-Deprived, and Miserable

Joanne Kimes
with Kathleen Laccinole

Technical Review by Leslie Young, M.D.

Aadamsmedia

Avon, Massachusetts

Published by
Adams Media, an F+W Publications Company
57 Littlefield Street, Avon, MA 02322 U.S.A.
www.adamsmedia.com

ISBN-10: 1-59337-627-8
ISBN-13: 978-1-59337-627-7

Printed in Canada.

J   I   H   G   F   E   D   C   B   A

Library of Congress Cataloging-in-Publication Data
Kimes, Joanne.
Bedtime sucks : what to do when you're both crying, cranky, and
miserable / by Joanne Kimes with Kathleen Laccinole ; with a technical
review by Leslie Young.
p.   cm.
Includes bibliographical references and index.
ISBN-13: 978-1-59337-627-7 (pbk. : alk. paper)
ISBN-10: 1-59337-627-8 (pbk. : alk. paper)
1. Bedtime. 2. Infants—Sleep. 3. Parent and infant. 4. Toddlers—Sleep.
5. Child rearing. 6. Parenting. I. Laccinole, Kathleen.
II. Young, Leslie. III. Title.
HQ784.B43K56 2007
649'.6—dc22
2007015783

This publication is designed to provide accurate and authoritative information with regard to the subject matter covered. It is sold with the
understanding that the publisher is not engaged in rendering professional
medical advice. If assistance is required, the services of a competent medical professional should be sought. The views expressed are solely those of
the author.
— From a *Declaration of Principles* jointly adopted by a Committee of the
American Bar Association and a Committee of Publishers and Associations

Many of the designations used by manufacturers and sellers to distinguish
their product are claimed as trademarks. Where those designations appear
in this book and Adams Media was aware of a trademark claim, the designations have been printed with initial capital letters.

The views expressed in this book are solely those of the authors.

This book is available at quantity discounts for bulk purchases.
For information, please call 1-800-289-0963.

To my mom, who, without the use of nannies, grammies, or witchcraft, was able to get two babies to fall asleep in the same room at the same time, and still manage to look fabulous.
—K.L.

To my sister, Laurie, who, unlike me, gave birth to a great sleeper. For that, I'll always be jealous of her for a change!
—J.K.

contents

acknowledgments

In every book I've written, I've given thanks to the usual list of suspects: my wonderful agent, Jeff Herman; my astute editors, Jennifer Kushnier and Meredith O'Hayre; my adorable husband, Jeff; and the girl of my dreams, my daughter, Emily. In this case, I'd also like to add my incredibly talented cowriter, Kathleen Laccinole, to the list.

But, in addition to these wonderful people, without whom this book would never have been written, I'd also like to thank you, the reader, without whom this book would never be read. And if it were never read, two things would happen: It would make all these months of typing just a foolish waste of time, *and* I'd have to give up being a writer, which is the best job a stay-at-home mom could dream of. So, I give you, the reader, a heartfelt thank you. (I wish I could throw in a 50 percent discount, but some things are out of my hands.)

I hope you enjoy the book!

introduction

If you're reading this book, you're no doubt dealing with the horrendous, life-altering, painful-as-a-Brazilian-bikini-wax aspect of parenthood. It's the age-old problem of getting your child to sleep, and it's a problem that has plagued sleep-deprived parents since the earliest life form crept out of the primordial ooze (or since Adam and Eve procreated for those of you who aren't into the whole evolution thing).

If you have a child with sleeping issues, you know firsthand how horrific life can be. In fact, these difficulties are to blame for sleep deprivation, forgetfulness, marital problems, mood swings, lack of focus, and of course, millions of vasectomies. In fact, when dealing with the problems of getting your kid to sleep, it suddenly becomes clear to you why some parents go out for a pack of cigarettes and never come back. I myself was tempted to do so on numerous occasions, and I'm not even a smoker (although I was tempted to start on numerous occasions as well).

That's because getting your kid to sleep is filled with enough challenges, dilemmas, and strategies to fill a book, which is exactly what I'm going to do right here and now. And although some of you lucky parents may have only one or two challenges to deal with, many of you will have to deal with most of them at one time or another between your child's newborn and toddler stages.

I'm not saying this to scare you. I'm actually saying it to make you feel better. The only thing that's worse than dealing with sleeping problems is thinking that you're the only one who's dealing with them. Having a kid who has trouble getting to sleep and staying that way is as common as buying a new computer and having it become obsolete the minute you get home.

As you go through this difficult phase of parenting, I wish you two things. One, that you find this book to be filled with many useful tips, helpful hints, and loads of laughs to get you through these trying times. And two, that you're so exhausted and numb to the pain that severe sleep deprivation can bring that you'll remain in a deep fog until your kid can sleep through the night. On that note, happy reading and pleasant dreams!

chapter 1

prelude to a kid

When you look at most baby sleeping help books, you'll notice that they begin their journeys immediately after the baby is born. But I'm going to do something a little different here. For no extra charge, I'm going to deal with the problems even earlier than that. In fact, I'm going to start talking about it at pregnancy. That's because, as every pregnant woman knows, getting eight hours of continuous sleep is nearly impossible. Your feet ache, your back hurts, you haven't pooped in a week, and your fetus is up partying more than Lindsay Lohan before she went to rehab. In most instances, the further along you are in your pregnancy, the more Mother Nature, jokester that she

1

is, teases you with sleepless nights. Some believe she's just giving a preview of what life is like after childbirth, but I think she's seeking revenge for that nasty hole we put in her ozone layer.

If you're still pregnant and going through this wretched stage of sleepless nights, I wish I had some words of wisdom to share. But alas, I don't. You'll just have to stick it out and know that one day, all the hell will be worth it. I know right now you think the only way it'll be worth your trouble is if your kid is born holding a pair of tickets to the *American Idol* finale, but believe me, it's true. Besides, no matter how exhausted you feel now, I promise that after the baby is born, you're going to feel a heck of a lot worse. Yes, if you think that pregnancy is exhausting, wait until you see how exhausted you are when your kid is on the outside!

Fortunately, there are some things you can do now to assure yourself more sleep later on. Along with going on your hospital tour and cleaning your house so well that it can safely house the Bubble Boy, there are some steps you can take in hopes of getting more shuteye. Even if you've already given birth, it may still behoove you to give this chapter a read. After all, as any good Girl Scout knows, it's good to be prepared. And now that the freckly faced Girl Scout is grown up and knocked up, you need to get preparing. So here are some basics ways to get your home ready so that the little one, and therefore the big ones, can get some sleep.

The Baby's Womb

If you and your partner are like those beautiful actor couples on Hollywood sitcoms, the decision as to where your baby will sleep has already been made for you. Your beautiful Gerber baby will sleep in a designer crib in your tiny, yet fabulously decorated bedroom, in an Upper West Side New York apartment. That's because the place is so small, there's nowhere else to put the little tyke (fodder for a later episode). You, with your sexy, never-been-pregnant body, and your gorgeous, face-like-a-Calvin-Klein-model mate will have quick, witty banter until your baby is awakened on cue. You'll then walk to the crib, trip over the perfectly trained dog, and make the studio audience erupt with laughter and applause (later to receive an Emmy for such a move).

But as you know, life so doesn't work this way. Fortunately most of us don't live in three-walled TV sets, so we have more options as to where to house our newborns. Deciding where your baby will sleep is one of the first things to obsess about after you've finally made that impossible decision of what to actually name your kid. By the way, if you haven't yet decided, don't stress. After reading all the books and having all the battles, all you ever call your kid is "Petunia" or "Junior" anyway (or "missy" or "mister" when they're bad).

The following list is made up of the most popular places where you can house your new baby. And while there are pros and cons to every choice, don't lament too much. That's because Petunia or Junior will no doubt move to several locations throughout the house, along with that hideous sculpture your mother-in-law gave you that you can never find a place for but must have on display at all times in case she pops by unannounced.

Your Bedroom

This is the place we've always imagined our newborn babies would be, probably because we've seen picturesque TV shows like the one previously mentioned. It's certainly the emotional choice, an idyllic tableau—you, your man, and your precious baby all slumbering together in one cozy room.

Along with this fantasy image, having your baby sleep in your room does have some practical advantages. For one, it's convenient, especially if you plan to nurse. Also, if Petunia is right there, your husband might be more inclined to pitch in and help. (Although don't count on it. The earlier you accept the fact that your spouse will never do as much as you do, the happier you'll be.) And finally, most new parents can't bear the thought of being so far from their precious bundles. What if something bad happens or she has her first hiccup or fart and they miss it?

While these are all valid reasons (except the fart thing because that's just plain weird), there are some downsides to this location. First off, babies aren't quiet. They're like little sports bars on Super Bowl Sunday. Also, while sex may be the furthest thing from your mind right now, you may want to have it again some day (well, your husband certainly will). And if you thought "doing it" with Fido staring at you was tough, you can forget about it when Junior is three feet away.

The Nursery
(also known as "The Baby's Room")
Putting a baby in his own room right from the get-go makes a lot of sense in the long run. The baby, while still as malleable as Play-Doh, gets used to his permanent surroundings right from the start. This aids in the establishment of

a healthy, long-term routine. And as every parent knows, a routine is a good thing. It prevents future trauma over uprooting your baby from your room and moving him to his own place. In my opinion, if you have the room, a nursery would be the most practical choice as to where your baby should sleep.

But when are new moms ever practical? Just look at that cashmere burp cloth you bought. If you can't imagine being down the hall from your newborn, maybe a compromise is the answer. Put a blow-up mattress in the baby's room and sleep there for a while. That way, he gets used to his own crib, and you're close by for feeding. Plus, you and your spouse can take turns caring for the baby so you can at least get half a night's sleep.

In the Nursery with a Night Nurse

Okay, this may sound like an opulent choice and one that's reserved for busy celebrities and members of the Trump family, but if you can afford it, it's a wonderful option. Especially if you've had a difficult delivery that included a C-section, a large episiotomy, or, hell, just pushing a kid the size of a broiler chicken out of your vagina. A night nurse is a professional you hire to come to your house in the evening and then leave in the morning when you're well rested and ready to take on another day's worth of challenges that come from having a newborn. You can arrange your night routine with your nurse however you choose, but generally she'll feed the baby (or bring Junior to you when it is time to eat if you're nursing and take him back to the nursery when you're finished). She'll change the diaper when necessary and gently rock him back to sleep so that you don't need to wake up at all.

While this all sounds good in theory, there are some downfalls to this system as well. To begin with, let's face it, can you really trust your bundle of joy to anyone except yourself? Most of us don't even trust our own husbands. Forget the fact that the nurse comes highly recommended, has raised ten kids of her own, worked in an ER, and has a Ph.D. in child care from Stanford University; this is *your* baby we're talking about!

Also, some people just don't like having extra people in their homes. Maybe they have a phobia about strangers using their toilets. Maybe they don't want to get caught with their faces in tubs of Ben & Jerry's at two in the morning. Or worse, find out that the nurse has eaten it all before they got there. Whatever the reason, bear in mind that a good night nurse is like a waiter in a busy restaurant and tends to be invisible. They're usually very good at respecting your privacy, giving you your space, and listening through the door before entering with Junior on the offbeat chance that you and your hubby are in the throes of passion, or more likely, throwing things at each other. (Don't worry. Fighting is a big part of parent-hood and causes more knockout brawls than *The Jerry Springer Show.*)

Aside from this, you also have a tremendous fear that your baby will bond with the nurse, rather than yourself. Not that this will ever hap-pen except for maybe those busy celebrities and members of the Trump family who's temporary night nurses turn into round-the-clock nannies who stay for eighteen years.

So while having a night nurse may seem like a luxurious choice, you may not want to go that route even if you can afford to. That is, of course, unless you're dealing with your second child. Par-ents are much more lax when dealing with sub-sequent children and would probably let Michael Jackson care for their children if it meant more sleep for them.

Baby on Board

Now that you've decided *where* your baby is going to sleep, you need to decide *what* device she will sleep in. Unfortunately, modern man, and modern baby stores, gives us way too many options. Not to worry. I'll break it down for you so that you can simplify your choice. The following are your most popular and most practical options for a baby sleeping container. The good news is that there really isn't a wrong decision. The bad news is that there isn't a right one either. That's because they're all wrong in one way or another.

A Bassinet

While these handy-dandy mini-cribs have been around for ages, they've had a recent resurgence in popularity with the advent of the Pottery Barn Kids catalog. What was once desirable only for its size and mobility is now coveted for its decorating aspects. Bassinets are convenient in that they don't take up much space, portable so that you can move your baby from room to room, small and therefore more comfortable for a newborn who prefers close quarters, and most important, cute as a bug in a rug! I have an idea. Let's forget the baby and just get the bassinet!

The problem with the bassinet is that your kid will outgrow it faster than Dolly Parton outgrew her first training bra. Also, they tend to have deep walls. Combine that with the fact that a baby has a "falling reflex" that can go off when lowering her inside (see "Falling Head over Heals" on page 48), and you're in for deep doo-doo.

A Crib

Many experts believe that it's best to put a baby in a crib right from the chute for consistency's sake. Train the little devils from day one, and they'll have fewer sleeping problems down the road. After all, what do they know anyway? They've got nothing to compare it to. They've just spent the past nine months being crammed up in a space so small, they had to curl up like a California roll just to be able to fit.

In case you've never seen a newborn in a crib before, think of a pea in the middle of the Sahara Desert. Since babies are used to tight quarters, get a crib divider, which allows you to block off most of the crib, making your baby feel more secure.

The Family Bed

A family bed is where your baby sleeps in the cozy womb of your room, in the even cozier womb of your bed—with you. It is a womb within a womb, so to speak. This is obviously the bed of choice for your baby since he gets to be near you and his food supply. Most babies tend to sleep longer in family beds, and if you're nursing, you can simply roll over and pop a boob in his mouth, without having to break a REM cycle.

But the news isn't always good. Although many people have success, many more are up half the night worrying that they or their spouses will roll over their kids and flatten them like a cartoon character on asphalt, or they fear that their babies will smother, even though they've removed every pillow from the beds and are forced to sleep on their own matted-up hair. The American Academy of Pediatrics actually frowns on an infant sleeping in a family bed. They feel that there are numerous dangers to contend with, especially before the child has developed the muscle strength to roll over at will. Even if parents can get over these fears, they still may be awakened by their newborns' velociraptor-like nails that cut them up like bologna in a deli slicer.

Even if you can overcome all that, sleeping in a family bed sets up the most difficult scenario to upgrade. No kid wants to leave those secure confines, and if you continue with this arrangement too long, you can expect that one day your son, and his new wife, will be cuddling up between you.

A Co-Sleeper

This combination crib and bassinet is the latest invention in mommy marketing. It's designed to attach to the side of your bed so that your baby can sleep next to you in bed, but not in the bed itself, thus alleviating your safety concerns. Plus, the co-sleeper is ideal for nursing moms who can simply reach over and grab their hungry customers.

But while it may be great for nursing moms, it's a pain in the ass for dads who are mechanically challenged. That's because the directions for setting them up can be as complicated to understand as the whole good cholesterol/bad cholesterol thing. Plus, if your mattress has a wonderfully cozy pillow top, then you'll also have to purchase leg extenders so that the co-sleeper is level with your bed. And finally, as with any other expensive newborn gizmo, your kid will outgrow it very fast. Although it's never been proven, I have a theory that the more expensive the baby container you purchase, the faster your baby will grow. Therefore, if you purchase a trendy co-sleeper or a designer bassinet, you should expect your kid to grow faster than Kelly Clarkson's career.

Infant Car Seat
Having a newborn sleep in her car seat isn't nearly as picturesque as seeing her lie sweetly in an antique-finish crib with pink gingham sheets.

Yet, while a car seat may not be the most visually pleasant sleeping container, it certainly makes the most sense. Sleeping in a car seat somewhat mimics the position that your baby was in while in utero—that is to say, like a little roly-poly bug. Since there are so many new experiences for your newborn to face in the outside world, having her sleep as she did in utero may be a tremendous comfort.

But some doctors believe that sleeping in a car seat can deprive a baby of oxygen and don't recommend sleeping there until after he's old enough to support his head. Check with your pediatrician. My pediatrician, and many others, think it's fine. As far as I'm concerned, there are as many schools of thought by doctors as there are

66 My newborn would wake up every few hours in the crib, but one night he fell asleep in the car, so we carried him in his car seat and put it in our room. I panicked the next morning realizing that he didn't wake all night, and I was sure that he had died. I forced myself to check and yeah, he was 'dead' alright. Dead asleep!99

—Kelly

doctors in school, so always go with the one that feels right in your gut.

Sock Drawer

This was the bed of choice in all black-and-white, screwball comedies circa 1925, where clueless, yet stylishly dressed, new parents did not have the wherewithal to purchase cribs, and the babies were therefore forced to sleep in emptied-out sock drawers. Even today people still use sock drawers, but they're as reluctant to tell you about it as they are that their wonderful new perfume comes from the Mary-Kate and Ashley collection.

Surprisingly enough, a sock drawer may be a good bed of choice when you and your hubby are on a trip. (Why you are traveling with a new baby is beside the point.) Maybe you opted not to bring along the porta-crib since who can figure out how to open those things anyway? You discover that the hotel crib is filthy dirty, so you line the dresser drawer with various items of your wardrobe, and in she goes. Trust me, you'll get the best night's sleep you've had since preconception. For whatever reason, babies love to sleep in sock drawers. It could have something to do with the small size, or perhaps it's the pine smell, but in a pinch (or not) it is a viable, practical, and affordable option.

Proper Sleepwear

Let's start with the basics. As you know, what you wear to bed at night can directly affect your ability to fall asleep. When your mate gives you a black nightie complete with buckles, chain, and a lacy thong, you know it has absolutely nothing to do with getting a good night's sleep. And while babies don't have the same doohickeys on their sleepwear, they are equally, if not more, sensitive to things like hard buttons, tags, and stiff fabrics.

While designer jammies are oh-so-cute, babies aren't particular about the latest fashion trend. What they are particular about is soft fabrics. Cotton has always been my fabric of choice. It's natural, usually reasonably priced, generally hypoallergenic, and like your favorite pair of 501s, gets softer with every washing.

It's also important for a jammie to have easy access during diaper changes, especially if you're trying to change your kid in the middle of the night without waking him up. For newborns, the gunny-sac jammies are great. They're the ones that look like itty-bitty sleeping bags. Feetsy pajamas are another good choice. They're so tiny and cute that, in a pinch, they could be used as decorative brooches. I like both gunny-sac and feetsies because they keep kids warm at night without the use of blankets, which inevitably get pushed to the bottom of cribs while kids suffer from hypothermia. And, according to most child safety experts, blankets in cribs may pose breathing threats.

No matter what form of jammies you decide upon, there are two things to look out for. One, be aware of buttons, bows, snaps, or any hard object on the back. Since it is recommended that newborns sleep on their backs (which is another point of debate—see page 32), these things could feel as if they're sleeping on a pile of rocks. Two, make sure that the pajamas are flame retardant. No amount of cuteness and "ahhhs" make up for the fact that it could light up like a cherries flambé and pose a risk to your precious loved one. There'll be plenty of dangers later on when it's time for middle school.

Warm Sheets

If your baby is born in the winter and you live in a drafty house with cold plaster walls, you should check out the temperature of your baby's sheets. You can't expect your child to pull an all-nighter when she's sleeping on a sheet of ice. Simply stated, refrigerated sheets are not conducive for sleep.

One way to alleviate this problem is to use a hot-water bottle. I bet you've had one of those rubbery things hiding under your bathroom sink since the mid-1970s. Dust it off, fill it with hot water, and place it on your baby's sheets as bedtime approaches. Once the sheets are sufficiently warm, remove the hot-water bottle and put your baby to bed. (*Do not* forget to remove the hot-water bottle for obvious safety reasons. Besides, if it isn't removed, the bottle will cool down and your baby will feel as if she's sleeping with a dead fish. Dead fish are not conducive for sleep either.)

If you don't have a hot water bottle, you can use an electric heating pad to warm up the sheets, but I must vehemently and neurotically insist that you must *always* remove the heating pad prior to putting your baby down. Leaving grill marks on your kid is again, not conducive for sleep. If you're at all forgetful, and what new mom isn't, get yourself a heating pad that has an automatic shutoff.

By the way, once you've removed either the hot-water bottle or the heating pad from your kid's crib, be sure to put it on your back to relieve all of your new mommy aches and pains. Now *that* is conducive for sleep!

Warm Balls

The only thing worse than the cold shoulder is the cold tushy. If you don't believe me, just ask your newborn. As you've no doubt been instructed by your pediatrician, your birthing classes, your baby books, and the wonderful nurse at the hospital who gave you cold packs for your aching crotch, you're newborn's sweet tush is far too sensitive to clean with standard baby wipes. Instead, you must use a wet cotton ball to clean all the nooks and crannies in your baby's hindquarters. The problem is that using a cold, wet cotton ball is like wiping your kid's ass with an ice cube. Within seconds, he'll voice his distain loud and clear.

So instead of dipping the cotton ball in the cold bowl of water that you left on the changing table hours ago, you grab the baby, run to the bathroom in the middle of the night to use warm water instead. But, by the time the tap finally runs warm, your baby's not only wide awake, but he has grown old enough to have facial hair. So what's a haggard mom to do?

Do yourself, and your baby's bee-hind, a big favor and put a thermos full of warm—not hot—water on the changing table before bedtime. Then, in the middle of the night when you're

❝ During my baby shower, someone gave me a heated wipe warmer, and I thought it was the silliest thing. So I returned it and got something I thought was much more important like a classical music tape for infants. As soon as my son was born, I realized that the inventors of the wipe warmer are bigger geniuses than the guys who wrote the classical music. **❞**

—Laurie

coma tired, the house is pitch black, and your baby is still half asleep, simply dip the cotton ball inside the thermos, and you and your kid's heiny will both be warm and happy campers.

After a few weeks, your baby's skin will be as tough as George Hamilton's, and you can switch to regular diaper wipes. Although these will be much more convenient, they too can be cold. I know it sounds indulgent, but if your kid bolts awake each night when you wipe him down with a cold wipe, get yourself a diaper wipe warmer. While you're out, get two of them and plug the second one in your bathroom. After all, why should your kid have the only happy heiny in the house?

Final Check

You've read the books, consulted the relatives, and interviewed the strangers who would talk to you, and you have decided upon the "right" place for your baby and decorated it to within an inch of its life. Good for you! But there are a few more details to consider before you go into labor.

Stand in your baby's room and take a look around. Is it calming, or do you feel as if you're at a birthday party at Chuck E. Cheese's? Do the walls whisper "relax," "sleep," and "dream," or are they as blaring as an acid rock concert? Does the pastel-colored overhead mobile play a soft, soothing lullaby, or is it a wild circus extravaganza that blasts Beethoven's Fifth? Remember, this is the place where you want your baby to fall asleep, not do step aerobics. And while for you it might be the culmination of a lifetime of decorating dreams, this isn't about you. Trust me, in two months you'll paint the walls black if it means getting your kid to sleep better.

And speaking of paint, does the room smell like a fresh coat of Ralph Lauren Chelsea blue? If so, let's hope that your baby stays in the womb until his room has aired out. Besides being toxic, the odor of new paint could keep the baby awake. Personally, I get a headache whenever I'm around the stuff so it makes sense that an extra-sensitive newborn could too, despite the fact that he has nostrils the size of pinholes.

Next, feel the sheets on the baby's bed to make sure that they don't feel like cardboard. Many new sheets do. That's why it's important to wash them before setting them up. Just be sure to use fragrance-free, hypoallergenic laundry detergent, or else your kid could get a rash that would rival any seen at a free clinic. And that would definitely interfere with your baby's sleep!

Now go to the crib and count the number of toys that are in there. I know you've already built up a sentimental attachment to them and given each one a name, but get them the hell out of there. They're not particularly safe since they could hinder your baby's breathing. And besides, those adorable stuffed animals may be stimulating to your baby, and stimulation is not what you need in bed . . . well, your baby's bed anyway.

Next, check out the temperature in the baby's room. Is there an air-conditioning vent over the crib? Does the radiator have a broken knob? You don't want to put your baby in the coldest or hottest room of the house. The baby's room should be somewhere around sixty-eight degrees. Check your thermostat, and then check the temperature in the baby's room to see if it's comfortable.

Another good idea is to put a night-light in the baby's room. You don't want to crash into her crib in the middle of the night when you go to check on her (twenty times a night for that matter). Crashing into the crib tends to wake up a sleeping baby. Also, you'll want to illuminate the obstacle course of toys and clothes that will invariably accumulate on the baby's room floor faster than dust bunnies.

As you can see, there are many things that you can do ahead of time to assure a good night's sleep once the baby's born. Okay, maybe not a *good* night's sleep. A good night's sleep will come only after your kid's old enough to sleep through the night, finished dealing with night terrors, over the stage when he can only sleep with Mommy,

> **❝**We were having a terrible time getting my daughter to sleep and called in a 'sleeping expert.' Two hundred and five dollars later, the problem was solved—two hundred for the 'baby sleep expert' who came to our house and five dollars for a roll of duct tape that we used to cover the fu*°%ing vent in her room.**❞**
>
> —Katie

past the waking up in a bed full of pee during potty training, and done with his nocturnal growing pains that continue through adolescence. So I guess your only hope of getting a *good* night's sleep is after your kid moves out of the house. But by that time, you'll be up with hot flashes and the constant need to pee, so I guess your good nights are done for good!

chapter 2

and baby makes three . . . hours of sleep!

You did it. You gave birth. Congratulations to you! Not only do you have a new baby, but if you played your cards right, you have a vial of good prescription medication as well! Woo hoo!

Yes, after nine long months, you finally get to hold your bundle of joy, count his itty bitty fingers and toes, and gaze into those beautiful blue eyes . . . that is when his eyes are open. For now that your baby is born, all he ever wants to do is sleep! What's going on? Did you just give birth to one of those miraculous babies you hear about in urban legends who sleep through the night as soon as they're born?! I hate to burst your bubble,

but I need to tell you a little somethin'-somethin':
It's common for a newborn to sleep a lot during
the first weeks after delivery. After millions of
years of human reproduction, the system has been
honed to perfection, and babies sleep the most at
the same time that moms need to sleep the most
as well. As you can tell by your painful stitches
and shredded genitalia, your body's been through
a traumatic ordeal, and you deserve downtime.

The problem is that having a kid turns your
once calm home into happy hour at Hooter's.
Relatives fly in. Colleagues come over. Neighbors stop by. And even though your privates are
as tender as a porterhouse steak, you're expected
to entertain the masses. So, for the time being,
limit the crowd. Right now your newborn needs
to sleep. And even though you're jacked up on
adrenaline, you need to sleep too. But when your
two-week respite is over and your baby opens his
eyes, and never seems to shut them again, here are
some ideas on how to get more shuteye at night.

Night and Day . . . You Are One

New babies are notorious for confusing day and
night. They've been residing in pitch-dark wombs
without windows to let in the sun's shining rays.

Day and night had no meaning before and, unfortunately for you, they still don't. Thankfully, this is only a temporary condition, and babies tend to fall into a regular night-and-day schedule within the first couple of months after birth. In the meantime, dealing with this issue will seem like an eternity in hell. If you're impatient, okay desperate, and don't want to wait for nature to take its course, there are a few things that you can try to jump-start the process and move your baby out of his nocturnal party-boy mode.

First, clearly separate night from day. During the day, don't keep the house ridiculously quiet. Make some noise, talk on the phone, dance the Pata Pata. Then at night, keep things quiet. Put your baby down in a mellow room that's designated for nighttime sleeping. Don't plop him in a bassinet, in the middle of your den in the same exact spot you were playing tickle torture with him just an hour before. Then, once he's tucked in, turn off the lights so it resembles nighttime. Hopefully, even your brand-new baby will grasp this concept, despite the fact that he's yet to even grasp the concept that he has a face. Conversely, don't use blackout shades for a noontime snooze. If you've ever woken up in a darkened hotel room at one in the afternoon, thinking it was 7:00 in the morning, and panicked as you feared that you've just slept through the only flight out of town and away from your husband's family, then you know just what I'm talking about.

Keep middle-of-the night feedings brief and uneventful so that you won't wake up the baby completely. Or, wake yourself up completely either. Don't turn on the light or kiss her delicious tootsies. Who knows? With your new giant-sized boobs that make even Jessica Simpson look like Kate Hudson, you may be able to nurse your baby without taking her out of the crib! Just know that if you start any interaction, nighttime is over and playtime has begun—and then you're in deep and utter despair.

Also, be sure to keep your little lumpkin's bedtime ritual different from her naptime ritual. At night, give her a calming bath, put on her cozy jammies, and sing her a soft lullaby. During the day, just plop her down in her red-checked cotton jumpsuit, with the adorable matching headband and ruffled anklets. Oh, and just a side note, don't be surprised if you change your baby's outfit ten times a day in order to use all the adorable things you received as shower gifts and can't wait to see her wear. This is perfectly normal behavior.

Still, if all else fails and you're stuck waiting for your little loved one to work out the kinks in her biological clock, don't fret. Take comfort in knowing there are millions of bleary-eyed parents all over the world suffering right along with you. Some babies refuse to sleep at night and love to sleep all day. (In fact, I know some twenty-year-old babies who act the same way.) And for those of you who have spawned such youths, here is my top ten list of things to do in the middle of the night to put you out of your misery:

10. Call a friend in Europe.

9. Pay your bills that have been lying around for two months.

8. Write thank-you cards for the wedding presents you received two years ago. Forget the baby gifts. Never gonna happen.

7. Watch some chick flicks that you could never get your husband to see at the theater.

6. Have sex. (Ha! Just kidding.)

5. Talk with your spouse. (Ha! Kidding again.)

4. Take a bath. But don't fall asleep in the tub no matter how tired you are.

3. Watch Comedy Central. If you thought you were in love with Jon Stewart before, wait 'til you have a baby.

2. Go online and buy your mother a belated thank-you gift for staying up with you when you were a baby.

And drum roll please . . .

1. If you've made it to number one on this list
   and your kid still hasn't fallen asleep, raid
   your refrigerator. Go ahead, spoon out the
   peanut butter with your finger and make
   yourself a bread and frosting sandwich. No
   one's around to see except your baby, and
   I know she can keep a secret!

Sleeping Through Mealtime:
To Wake or not to Wake, That Is the Question

Generally (and I mean this in the broadest sense
of the word since all babies are different) newborns (and I mean from out of the chute until
three months of age) sleep a lot (and I do mean
a lot). The good news is that babies don't really
need to eat that much during the first few days.
This is another example of the perfectly honed
system since it usually takes that long for your
milk supply to come in (or for you to stock up
on formula). When your milk does comes in
(whether from breast or Costco), your baby wakes
up more, then eats more . . . then more, and more
. . . and more . . . until finally, your kid acts like
he's in training to be a contestant on *The Biggest*

Loser. This pattern of aggressive eating emerges during these first months of life, and whether you feed on demand or start a rigid schedule is up to you, your personality, your lifestyle, and your pediatrician's advice.

Still the question remains, what do you do if your baby is asleep at night and you've just woken up in a panic realizing it's been six hours since Junior's chowed down? Do you wake up your little darling or let him sleep? This is one of life's difficult decisions like, "would you like to supersize your order?"

The answer to this question isn't as clear-cut as the supersize thing since who in their right mind could pass up a bucket-size container of French fries? In this case, the deciding factor of whether to wake a sleeping baby is what your pediatrician believes. As you've learned during pregnancy, doctors have different beliefs about certain things. Some wouldn't allow you to take an extra-strength Tylenol for a headache, while others wouldn't think twice before prescribing strong migraine medication. On that same note, some pediatricians would say to wake up your baby every two hours so that he won't dehydrate, while other say to leave him be.

If your doctor suggests that you wake up your kid to eat, do so. But good luck. Chances are you'll have more frustrations than successes. For one thing, you'll have to set your alarm so that *you* can wake up to wake up your kid. Then you'll have to walk that fine line of waking him up just enough so that he'll eat, yet not too much that he won't be able to fall back to sleep when he's done.

If your kid can sleep for a six-hour stretch and your pediatrician says it's okay to let him sleep, savor the moment, and get some much needed rest. Oh, and keep the fact that you slept a six-hour stretch to yourself. Other, not-so-fortunate new parents, will never forgive you.

Belly Up

Would you believe that if you had your baby a mere generation ago, your doctor would have advised you to put your newborn on his stomach when it was time for beddie bye? Back then, people didn't worry about SIDS (sudden infant death syndrome) because there wasn't much to know about it (the term wasn't even thought up until 1968). So, instead of new parents stressing out that their kids could stop breathing, they instead panicked that they would spit up during the night and choke on their own vomit. (New parents always have *something* to worry about.)

SIDS is the leading cause of death in infants under one year of age, and although there is much confusion as to why it occurs (it may be linked to the awakening system) or if it's genetic or not, experts agree that the number of deaths can be reduced if infants are put to sleep on their backs. The belief is that by doing this, they'll be able to breathe better than they would if put on their stomachs.

Some babies don't seem to mind being put down on their backs. They lie there as if they're poolside at the Beverly Hills Hotel awaiting their mai tais. But most others find the position to be quite uncomfortable and therefore don't sleep very well. And as all exhausted parents know, when their babies don't sleep well, nobody does.

As frustrating as this scenario is, you understand the reason behind it. SIDS is a tragic occurrence, made even more prevalent if you smoked or used drugs during pregnancy, use drugs now, were younger than twenty at the time your baby was born, or if your baby was born early or is of a low birth weight. (For the complete list of vulnerabilities, go to *www.sids.org.*) Since parents started putting their kids to sleep on their backs, there has been more than a 40 percent drop in the amount of deaths due to SIDS from 1992 to 1995. Oddly enough, there has been a 90 percent increase in parents who are at their wit's end because their kids aren't sleeping well. If you're one of these exhausted, up-all-night parents, here are some things that you can do to try to get your newborn to sleep for a longer stretch of time:

- Swaddle her up good and tight. Often a baby put to sleep on her back will startle more often as she relaxes to sleep. This, of course, will wake her, and then you, up.
- Put your baby to sleep on his side. Some newborns find this position to be more comfortable, but keep in mind that there is debate as to the safety of this as well. Therefore, be sure to get your pediatrician's okay first. To keep your baby in place, lay him down between some rolled-up receiving blankets or in a specially designed device that holds him like a wiener in a hot dog bun. But the safety of these props is debatable since they may pose a breathing concern. Again, check with your pediatrician first.
- Get yourself an Angelcare monitor. It's a monitor that goes underneath the mattress and picks up the breathing sounds of your baby. If he stops breathing, an alarm sounds. True, it won't get your baby

to sleep any longer, but since it will ease your worries, it may allow you to get more shuteye!

Fortunately, once your newborn is a few months old and has the muscle strength to flip himself over like a buttermilk pancake, all bets are off. At that time he can roll over at will, sleep on his stomach if he pleases, and it's out of your hands!

"Growth Spurts" Is not Only an X-Rated Movie

After months of sleepless nights, you finally have your new baby on a decent schedule. She eats, plays, and naps in predictable cycles. She even sleeps several hours straight at night. You brag to your mommy group, your family, and all of your neighbors. You even think about having sex again (don't worry, you don't actually have to do it). You feel like you've made it through the worst part of the storm and there's nothing but clear skies and slumbering nights ahead! You haven't been this happy since they came out with a low-fat version of cookie dough ice cream.

But then out of nowhere, black storm clouds appear. Without notice, your baby backpedals and wants to eat almost every hour. Not only that, but she's up half the night crying from hunger. If you're nursing, you worry that there's something wrong with your milk supply. Have your new gravity-defying ta-tas been sucked dry? Or maybe your baby has picked up a tapeworm? Crap, you knew you shouldn't let Fluffy sleep in her crib. Okay now, before you go crazy, stop right there. Your breasts are fine (and beautiful, might I add), and your baby doesn't have a tapeworm. You've just discovered the hell of dealing with a growth spurt.

Most babies go through surges in appetite around the ages of three weeks, six weeks, nine weeks, and three months. Luckily for breastfeeding mothers, your breasts won't run out of milk because they work on supply and demand, not unlike the Tickle Me Elmo sensation of 1996. The more your baby sucks, the more milk your breasts produce. When your baby grows, he needs more food to feel full and thrive. Ergo, he is hungrier. Ergo, he nurses more. Ergo, your breasts create a new supply of milk to keep your larger baby healthy and content. And ergo and ergo it goes.

This situation is far easier to deal with if you're bottle-feeding since all you need to do is add more milk in the bottle. But if you're breastfeeding, growth spurts can cause you quite a lot of grief until your breasts figure out their new production schedule. You can try feeding your baby more during the day if she'll let you in hopes of sustaining her more at night, but good luck with that. You can bring a baby a nipple, but you can not make him suck.

The good news is that growth spurts are truly just that—little "spurts" of time. The whole shebang usually lasts a few days. Then you have the fun of "re-establishing" that fantastic schedule you were bragging about just three days before. Remember, a growth spurt is totally normal, good even, as it indicates that your baby is growing. I know this probably doesn't offer much comfort to someone who's been up two nights straight with an infant for a nipple ring, but take a deep breath, be patient, and focus on the important things: like that low-fat cookie dough ice cream!

We All Know People Who've Done It . . . Okay, Okay, We've All Done It!

All the books tell you not to feed your baby to sleep. Your pediatrician tells you not to do it, your friends tell you not to do it, and your mother tells you not to do it. In fact, feeding your kid to sleep is about as shunned upon in our society as

marrying your first cousin. You know you're supposed to teach your baby to fall asleep by herself, and you fear that if anyone finds out, they'll
call child protective services and have your baby
yanked from your loving arms.

The problem is that these people have never
met your child. They have no idea how impossible it is to get your little tax deduction to la-la
land, or how exhausted and cranky you are. They
don't understand that you haven't showered in
days, haven't slept more than two consecutive
hours since giving birth, and that you're one step
away from abandoning your family and running
off with the mailman, who may be in his sixties,
but at least doesn't judge your parenting skills.

But I'm here to tell you otherwise. If you
want to feed your infant until she falls asleep, you
go right ahead and do it. (This is assuming that
she doesn't have teeth yet, in which case don't. It
could cause tooth decay!) In fact, I'm here to say
that all those perfect people who are telling you
not to do it have most assuredly done it themselves! Come on, folks. Step out of the closet. It's
nothing to be ashamed of. All the cool moms are
doin' it! Let's just join forces and admit to the
world that we're all human, well, semihuman
anyway, because we're all just a few hours shy of
falling asleep standing up.

With that said, I do want to put out a cautionary piece of advice: Feeding a baby until she falls asleep is like using a vibrator. It's fine to do on occasion but should not be made a habit. Once the addiction takes place, breaking it will be nearly impossible and can be very hard on your baby . . . or your sex life depending on the addiction you're trying to break.

Another problem with feeding your kid until she falls asleep is that you could actually be *teaching* her to fall asleep while she's eating. It's the old Pavlovian dog and pony show: Your kid learns that whenever she gets a nipple in her mouth, it's time for lights out. Then, if she conks out when she eats, she won't fill up her belly and will snack throughout the day. Not only will she wake up hungry in a couple of hours, but she'll learn to be a snacker and will spend the rest of her life sustaining on a steady stream of Chex Mix and peanut butter–filled pretzels.

If you find yourself with one of these tykes who nods off during mealtime, there are a few things that you can try to keep her up so you can fill her up. (Note: The following also applies to your spouse.)

1. Talk to your baby. A little bit of encouragement might help.

2. Try a little jiggle, but not a shake. *Never shake your baby.*

3. Stroke the bottoms of his feet or the palms of his hands.

4. Tickle the side of his cheek to jump-start the rooting reflex.

5. If you're desperate, try taking off his clothes. (This one will definitely work on your spouse.)

The bottom line is that you want your baby to learn to fall asleep without the need of the bottle or the boob. But if he simply refuses, a good compromise would be to feed him until he's *almost* asleep, and then put him to bed to fall asleep the rest of the way by himself. This way, your kid will still learn to fall asleep by himself, and you'll be far less desperate. The only one who gets screwed in this scenario is your sixty-year-old mailman. But he needs more naps than your baby does, so forget about him.

Routines Are a Good Thing

Most of us don't like surprises. We've had enough of those during pregnancy, thank you very much, when we developed a third nipple, errant moles, and filled up with more gas than an Exxon station. We like to know what's coming next, and babies are no different in this department. In fact, they crave routine more than we crave Double Stuf Oreos. So if you want to get your kid to fall asleep, you need to establish a nighttime ritual for your baby that culminates in—you got it—falling asleep!

Might I suggest the five Bs: **b**ath, **b**ottle, **b**urp, **b**ook, **b**ed. You can throw in a **bm** too, if you like. (It stands for **b**aby **m**assage . . . although a BM would help if you ate too many of those Oreos.) Yes, a baby massage is trendy, but it's also adorable, fun, and does help your little tyke to relax. (See "Resources" on page 195 for instructions.) Just don't let your hubby see you do it, or else he'll want equal time, and rubbing his pimply, hairy back won't be quite as adorable.

Bear in mind that the five B plan is a well thought-out and mommy-tested system. For instance, it's a good idea not to put the **b**ottle or **b**oob right before **b**ed or else your child may not be able to fall asleep *without* the **b**ottle or **b**oob. Also, notice that there's nothing in the list that can cause you future misery. For instance, there's no **B** for **b**oombox that you can forget on a trip or **B**arney CD that can get so repetitive you end up throwing it hard against the wall.

When it comes to the **b**ook selection, you need to be smart. Get books that are soft and relaxing, with pastel pictures of fuzzy bunnies or some such fluff. Also, be careful how you read these books. A Vincent Price rendition of *Pat the Bunny* will not set up the mood for night-night.

Whatever routine you establish, realize that you'll be sticking with it for some time. Then, as your kid ages, the **b** for the **b**oob or **b**ottle will be replaced by the **b** for the **b**rushing of the teeth. At some point down the road, the only thing that your bedtime ritual will consist of is a hug and a kiss good night. Of course, when that day comes, it'll be very **b**ittersweet. **B**itter because it means that your child doesn't need you as much, but sweet because it won't take an eternity to put him to bed so you can finally catch an episode of *Lost* like everyone else in the world! And that is a **b**eautiful thing!

chapter 3

the hand that rocks the cradle . . . is exhausted

Okay, so you're not Supermom after all. You're baby is up during the night, and your spirits are down during the day. You're tired and cranky and covered in dried puke. You're also resentful of your spouse. (Yup, that doesn't end now that the whole pregnancy ordeal is over.) He's lingering over a business lunch while you're stuck at home with a kid who just peed in your mouth during a diaper change. Your nipples have blisters, your hemorrhoid just burst, and your postpartum depression finally kicked in. You'd cry in frustration, but you know you'd just pee in your pants (a lovely aftereffect of childbirth!). You'd give your right arm to have three consecutive hours of sleep, and your left one to have your roots done. To put it bluntly, you're losing it, girl!

So, in hopes of getting more shuteye, your new goal in life, let's deal with some frustrations you may face when getting your little one to sleep. Some are only mildly annoying, others make you want to scream, and a few cause you to rethink the whole child-rearing thing and raise alpacas instead.

Raising a Baby the Write Way

You knew having a baby would bring you lots of fulfillment and joy, but did you know it would bring tons of paperwork as well? It seems that along with the bulk-sized container of diapers and cans of formula, a new parent also needs to have reams of paper on hand to chart, graph, and log every movement of their babies' lives. Yes, when you have a baby, you become Dian Fossey, and your baby is a gorilla in the mist.

Chances are you already have a chart going that maps your child's eating habits. Not only do you have to graph out what goes into your baby, you most likely also have to keep track of what comes *out* of her as well. Each dirty diaper has to be made note of in intricate detail.

Now, on top of all this time-consuming paperwork comes a new chart that all the trendy moms are doing. This is the chart that keeps track of your baby's sleeping habits. The belief behind this madness is that if you have an accurate account of your baby's sleeping habits, you can gauge whether or not your child is sleeping better and what you can do to help her sleep more. If you thought the eating and pooping log was time-consuming, wait'll you catch a peek at the sleeping log! *Logs*, in fact, because there are actually three of them if you're following the current trend: a napping log, a night-waking log and a pre-bedtime log. (See "Resources" on page 198 for full details . . . or better yet, don't!)

I say forget all the paperwork and get back to the important stuff like remembering to turn off the stove when you leave the house. Medieval-mama did not need charts and graphs. Prairie-mama did not need charts and graphs. And you, after your second child, will not need charts and graphs. As long as your pediatrician says that your baby is thriving as he should, relax. Take back the time that you would be writing, and have some time for yourself. And about keeping a log of dirty diapers? Forget about it! You have

way more important things to do than caring
about a bowel movement. You'll be doing plenty
of that in your geriatric years.

Past the Point of No Return

You and your little one are in a pretty good
groove now. You can recognize all of her basic
needs such as hunger, comfort, and the desire
to put everything in her mouth. At the end of
your long day, you notice that Petunia is doing
the double whammy of the yawn slash eye rub,
so you swing into full bedtime mode. Everything's going according to plan when suddenly,
the doorbell rings. It's your neighbor holding a
homemade red velvet cake. Not wanting to be
rude (and after all, it is cake), you invite her in.
Although this distraction may satisfy your sweet
tooth, it doesn't satisfy your baby's need to sleep.
Once your neighbor leaves, you try to put her
down, but the window of opportunity for sleep
has been slammed shut, and your baby is officially overtired.

　　Yes, once a baby gets overtired, he finds it
impossible to unwind. There's no infant version
of a glass of Merlot and a *People* magazine to relax
with. So what do babies do instead? That's right,

they *cry*. And cry and cry and cry, which only serves to wind them up even further until they've sunk into an abyss so deep, they can only get out of it with the help of those jetpacks they had on the *Jetsons* that you thought would be commonplace by now.

The lesson here is that you need to have an amazing excuse for not putting your kid to bed when he's tired like . . . well, I can't think of anything. Nothing is worth the hell of dealing with an overtired baby. No late-night videos (unless it's the latest Brad Pitt film) or late-night dinner (unless it's with Brad Pitt himself).

Some parents make the misguided mistake of keeping their sleepy babies awake during the day in hopes of getting them to sleep longer at night. *Wrong!* An overtired baby will sleep even less at night. Interestingly enough, babies who sleep well during the day tend to sleep better at night. The big lesson to learn is that *sleep begets sleep*. And as you know, the better Junior sleeps, the better senior sleeps as well.

Once your kid is overtired, there's not much to do but wait it out. What you shouldn't do however is swing, play, watch videos, listen to loud music, or put him in one of those vibrating bouncy chairs that we all wish came in our size. None of these methods work and may even

make matters worse. Overtired babies are generally overstimulated babies so the key here is to
un-stimulate them.

Take your baby into a quiet room; dim the
lights; speak in hushed, soft tones; sing a soft
lullaby; and let her scream it out. And as difficult as it sounds, stay calm. If things get bad,
and she's beyond the point of no return, feed her.
Yes, I know that using food to destress a baby
will eventually lead to the freshman fifteen, but
you're desperate here. Besides, after she's asleep,
you can de-stress too . . . with the rest of that
yummy cake!

Falling Head over Heals

Your baby's exhausted but isn't falling asleep.
You've paced back and forth so many times that
you've worn a hole in your sock, your shoe, and
the hardwood floor. Finally, after all that effort,
you've gotten your little loved one to fall asleep
in your arms. Ever so gingerly, you lean over the
edge of the crib and lower her down on the mattress when—WHOA—out of nowhere, she flings
her arms and legs out to the side and screams hys-
terically as if you're tossing her into the Grand
Canyon. Now she's wide-awake, kicking and

yelling like never before, and you're thinking, "What the heck did I do wrong?" (Actually, your dialogue is much more R-rated, but we want to be able to sell this book at all the major stores.)

The answer, my poor pathetic pooped-out parent, is that you did nothing wrong. You're just dealing with one of the most horrific aspects of putting a baby to sleep: the Moro reflex (also known as the startle reflex). As you may know, babies are born with a veritable smorgasbord of fascinating and fun reflexes and responses. Stroke the sole of your baby's foot and his toes flare out. Stroke her cheek, and she roots and turns her head to look for a nipple. Poke your finger into the palm of Baby's hand, and he'll grasp it and close his fingers around it like a sea anemone. You could play with these reflexes for hours. It's like you've given birth to an eight-pound Game Boy.

But the reflex that holds absolutely no enjoyment at all is the Moro reflex. This is the one where a loud noise or the sensation of falling will cause a baby to flail and be startled. And when that baby is falling asleep, it'll cause her to go from relaxed to hysterical in .6 seconds. This reflex is a part of our human machinery that Mother Nature hasn't quite worked the kinks out of yet. The belief is that back when we were furry creatures roaming Earth and Mamma Cave Monkey would drop her

> **"** Whenever I'd lower my infant into her bassinet,
> she'd always flail awake. Eventually, I perfected the
> art of lowering her in ever so slowly and carefully
> that she'd stay asleep. I felt as if I was putting a
> container of nitroglycerine to bed. **"**
>
> —Marie

offspring, this instinct would cause her young to instantly reach up and grab her furry body. But now with the aid of evolution and the Lady Schick shaver, we're no longer furry creatures. Nevertheless, the Moro reflex remains.

If you're dealing with this reflex, there are a few things you can do to keep it Moro or less to a minimum:

1. When you lower your sleeping baby into her crib or bassinet, keep her as close to your body as possible for as long as possible. Hug her while you gradually bend over and contort yourself into a position that's donned the cover of several girly magazines. Then place your baby on her mattress before you actually relinquish contact with your body.

Once a slumbering baby feels a mattress on her back, she usually feels secure enough not to flail.

This is where being tall really works in your favor (as well being able to wear those adorable Capri pants). Tall girls can gracefully pirouette to the cribs, lean over in a perfect yoga forward bend, and place their babies on the mattresses without so much as a flinch. Shorter women have more of a challenge doing this feat (and looking good in Capris. I should know. I'm short.) If it helps, make sure that you have the mattress on its highest rung. (Remember to lower the mattress as your baby grows.)

2. Swaddle your baby up tightly. (See "Resources" on page 196.) There's something about being snugly contained that gives a baby a sense of comfort and security. If you've ever had an herbal wrap at a spa, you know exactly what I mean. Also, when you wrap your baby up in a blanket, her arms can't flail around because they're locked up as well as Mark David Chapman.

3. Lie down on the floor and feed your baby to sleep. Okay, so you're desperate. You haven't slept in days. You're convinced that your kid is implanted with a high-tech,

sci-fi sensor that reacts every time you lower her. Give yourself a break and lie down on the floor, feed your kid to sleep, close the door so Fido or Fluffy can't get in, then leave (or fall asleep yourself). No flailing necessary.

How Much Sleep Does This Little Thing Need Anyway?

This is the thing; there are a bazillion charts and graphs in every baby book on the market telling you how much sleep your baby needs based on his age, weight, height, and your SAT score. Aside from the charts in the how-to baby manuals, your pediatrician will also give you some sort of guideline, which I'm confident you'll be far too tired to comprehend as well.

Personally, I think it's all a bunch of hooey. There is no one-and-only answer as to how much sleep your baby is going to need. You may have a sleepy baby, an average baby, or a cat-nap baby. It's in their wiring along with the wave in their hair, the color of their eyes, and how old they'll be when they ask, "Mommy, where did I come from?" One baby may sleep all the time (my dream baby), and still another might hardly sleep at all (my actual baby).

One general rule of thumb that may dictate how much sleep your baby will need is how much food he takes in. The older the baby, the better eater he'll be. The better eater he'll be, the more food he can hold, and the longer he can sleep without waking up hungry. Of course, it also helps if you're bottle-feeding. Formula is thicker and tends to stick to the ribs. Breastmilk is like milk whereas formula is like a milkshake.

So the question we must ask ourselves here is not how much sleep does your baby need to thrive, but rather how much sleep does your baby need for *Mommy* to thrive. After extensive scientific research and several minutes of thinking up jokes, the following table has been created:

Baby's Age	Approximate Hours of Sleep Needed	Mom's Response
Newborn	16–20 hours	You're getting enough rest to be okay. Plus, you're jacked up on pain meds so although you may be a little bit tired, you don't really give a crap.
1 month	18 hours	You're exhausted and up all night. You fight with your husband all the time and think he's a total loser.

Baby's Age	Approximate Hours of Sleep Needed	Mom's Response
6 months	15–18 hours	You hardly sleep at all. You left your cell phone on the roof of your car. You almost left your kid up there too. so things could be worse.
1 year	15 hours	You're still up once or twice a night, but your body's adjusting. Your husband's looking good to you again, but secretly, you're in love with one of the brothers on *Zoboomafoo*. You can't tell them apart so you don't know his name, which makes it even hotter.

Why Husbands Should Be Destroyed

Daddies. They come in all shapes, sizes, and colors. They offer loads of help manning grills, taking out the trash, and reaching the stuff on high shelves. But when it comes to getting babies to sleep, the only thing they offer is truckloads of grief. In fact, Daddies are actually baby insomnia with a five o'clock shadow.

Picture this: You've been dealing with your kid solo since 8:00 in the morning when your husband went off to work (after having a full night's sleep, by the way, so that he could be fresh for the office). All day it's been nonstop nursing, changing, crying, and struggling to get your kid down for his naps. In between you've dealt with the house, the pets, the errands, the shopping, all in a zombie-like state (or you've been working hard at the office and still have to deal with all that crap).

Now it's 7:00 at night, and you've fed, bathed, and read to your baby, and you are watching her drift off to sleep, when ta-da, Daddy's back! He slams the door, throws down his briefcase, and hollers "I'm home!" loud enough for the space shuttle astronauts to hear. Wanting to spend some time with the fruit of his loins, he stomps into the baby's room, scoops up his kid, and tosses her into the air like pizza dough. Now your child's wide-awake, and you'll be up until midnight getting her back to sleep.

If this scenario sounds the least bit familiar, don't feel bad, you're not alone. Daddies are an unexplainable phenomenon, like UFOs or Yanni's enormous fan base. Countless Mommies around the world suffer the same complaint.

If this situation is a problem for you, either delay your baby's bedtime so that it's after Daddy comes home, or consider one of the following options.

Option one Talk to your husband. Beg and plead; speak logically and patiently; and employ diagrams, graphs, and the words of experts and elders to convince your man that he should not stimulate a sleepy baby.

Option two Accept it. Realize that Daddy feels guilty that he's been gone all day and wants to spend a little quality time with his kid. Sure, you wish quality time meant a lullaby instead of a mosh pit, but men show their paternal love in a more physical and playful manner.

Option three Tell Daddy that if he overstimulates the baby, then he has to be the one to get the baby to sleep. My guess is that once he sees the enormous challenge it is to deflate an overinflated energetic baby, he'll change his ways.

If You Thought Housewives Were Desperate, You've Never Seen a Tired Mom

Forget trickle-down economics; the real trickle-down theory applies to the home. And contrary to what you may think, your baby is not at the top of the triangle—*you are*. If you're a basket case, it's going to affect your milk supply, your mood, your marriage, your body, and your ability not to murder your husband when he takes out a bottle of frozen breastmilk that took you four days to pump, and forgets about it, leaving it to ruin on the counter overnight.

I know you're exhausted and want to escape it all by driving to another state, but that didn't work for Marie Osmond, and it's not going to work for you either. You've got to get some rest, and you've got to get it *now*! If you don't, the walls of your world could come tumbling down. Repeat after me, "I am Mommy; hear me snooze." For goodness' sake—if you can birth a baby and figure out how to hook together that damn BabyBjörn, you can arrange to get some much-needed shuteye. Here are some ideas on how you can make it happen:

- Put your husband on the couch and keep the baby with you. If your husband snores, this tip alone should double your amount of REM sleep!
- Sleep when your baby sleeps. (Ha, right! Just thought I'd throw that in for a laugh!)
- Instead of having your girlfriends take you out to lunch for your birthday, ask them to go in on a gift certificate for Merry Maids.
- Make a policy that anyone who wants to come over to see the baby must bring a

turkey meatloaf and side of mashed potatoes so you don't have to cook that night.

- Get over yourself, and ask any and all of those who love you for some help. They will. They want to. And it's good for your child to get used to different people. After all, these are the people he will grow to love as well.

- Let your mother-in-law help. Yes, I know it goes against everything you stand for, but these are desperate times. You can always go back to your usual animosity once the baby sleeps better.

- Tell your husband that if he doesn't take your baby on a *long* walk, you'll file for divorce and give him full custody.

The Best-Laid Plans of Mice and Babies

Everything you thought you wouldn't do—you are. Everything you thought would happen—isn't. You need to reassess the situation and rethink your sleeping strategies. And that's okay. In fact, it's completely normal. As far as I'm concerned, parenting is nothing but an exercise in improvisation that'll leave even the best stand-up comic speechless.

Before I brought my daughter home from the hospital, I had an amazing game plan: I'd lay her down in the family bassinet that was passed down through generations. My husband and I would stare at our little miracle for hours and then make mad, passionate love. After a week, when my daughter was able to sleep through the night, I'd move her into a nursery that was so gorgeous, it would put Martha Stewart to shame. At the end of our fulfilling day, I'd lay my angel down in her crib where she'd drift off to sleep, only to awaken twelve hours later, just as I finished my morning coffee.

If you're not laughing now, just wait. It gets even better: I would breastfeed my child for a year, after which she'd happily switch to the bottle, or perhaps being as gifted as she'd be, go directly to the cup. I would write during the day while she napped—three hours in the morning and two hours in the afternoon. And when she was awake, she would play happily for hours on the floor by my desk on her educational activity mat. Of course, my husband and I would continue to have our nights out, and I would continue to go to the gym so that I could get my pre-pregnancy figure back in three months flat.

Ha! The only part of my fantasy that ever came true was that my daughter did indeed start

off in a family bassinet, but that didn't last long
because my husband threw it against the wall
since she'd flail awake whenever he'd lower her
inside. Everything else, all lies!

My point is that parenting is not about perfection. You might start out one way, then change
your mind midstream. The key is to relax. If your
standards are too high, if you're too rigid, you're
only setting yourself up for failure. Don't be so
hard on yourself if you're doing exactly what the
baby books say and you're not getting the result
you want. Your kid isn't a leaky faucet that needs
to be repaired. (Okay, she does leak from time to
time, but that's beside the point.) Just keep trying until you find what works for you and your
baby.

> **"**After I had my baby, people were always amazed at
> how quickly I was able to fit back into my pre-pregnancy
> clothes. Little did they know how exhausted I was from
> not sleeping and how stressed out I was over my marital
> problems. Those two conditions combined made for a
> quicker weight loss than Atkins.**"**
>
> —Barbara

On that note, don't stress too much about the things that aren't getting done. Your kid loves you with your dirty laundry and your messy hair. And beside, your rarely shaved armpits and legs will keep your sexually deprived hubby at bay! Accept the fact that you'll never be able to accomplish all the things you used to do before you had a child. And that's okay. I'm sure you'd rather have a precious miracle than a pine-scented floor any day!

If you do ever manage to create a semblance of order in your overhauled life, and your baby sleeps six hours a night and you have a nap schedule that every other Mommy at Gymboree covets, it's all going out the window as soon as Baby cuts her first tooth, or you take a vacation, or daylight-saving time arrives, or your kid gets the sniffles, and so on and so on and so on! So take deep breath, take it day by day, and *don't* take it all so seriously!

chapter 4

sleeping aids

Time has passed, your baby's grown bigger, and so have your frustrations. Sure, you know how to deal with growth spurts and can now swaddle your newborn like baby origami, but you still can't get your kid to fall asleep when you want her to, especially during the day. Like any new challenge, you just have to keep with it. There are still plenty of avenues to explore in hopes of getting your schnuckums to sleep . . . and to keep her that way. You just have to find your "it"—the thing that works for you and your baby.

But, after lots of exhausting trial and error, when you finally do discover your "it" revel in your success.

A child is like the weather in Hawaii and can change every five minutes. So, in hopes of unlocking the clues to your "it," let me offer some tried-and-true ways to send your baby off to dreamland. You may notice that many of these remedies are the result of modern-day technology and weren't around a mere century ago. I hope this'll make you appreciate living in these times and make dealing with crap like frozen computers and dropped cell phone calls much easier.

Baby, Won't You Drive in My Car?

Any new mother will attest to the fact that taking a baby for a spin in the car is a foolproof way of getting him to sleep. We can all relate to the soothing effect a running motor can have on the conscious mind. How many of us have woken up on airplanes in midsnort, horrified to find our heads on our neighbors' chests? Babies are no different and are, in fact, even more sensitive to the droning seduction of a car engine. Not only does driving provide great comfort to your infant, but it also provides great comfort to you. Your car is a safe haven where you can get away from your messy house and laugh at callers on the *Dr. Laura* show who think they have big problems that actually pale in comparison to yours.

But with every good, there is a bad, and driving with a sleeping kid is not without its problems. For one thing, it's akin to that movie *Speed* where Sandra Bullock and Keanu Reeves have to keep that bus in motion, or else it'll blow up. For you too will find a disastrous ending if your car ever stops moving: Your kid'll wake up!

If you go out for a drive so that your kid can catch a few hours of z's, don't forget to bring along some snacks. Otherwise, if you get hungry, you'll be forced to play the ever-so-dangerous game of Drive-thru Russian Roulette where you have to maneuver your car ever so slowly so that it never comes to a complete stop. If it does, you're dead.

Although using your car is a safe and effective way to get your kid to sleep, use it sparingly as you would any other addictive substance. It's a bad habit to get into and should be used only in emergencies, like when you're visiting your in-laws and your baby can't nap because the house is filled with relatives and you're forbidden to stay at a hotel because your husband says it would hurt his mother's feelings despite that fact that you're on the edge of a nervous breakdown. Also be aware that if your kid is sleeping in the car, and you don't want to spend a fortune in gas, or further pollute our environment while your child takes a three-hour nap, you'll have to attempt the car-to-crib transfer, a move that can be even more dangerous than Drive-thru Russian Roulette.

Babies Suck . . . and Suck . . . and Suck . . . and Suck

One of the best ways to get your kid to sleep is to stick something in his mouth. There's just something about sucking that relaxes a person . . . especially if that person is short, bald, and toothless with no inhibitions about pooping and farting. (No, I'm not talking about your husband.)

The problem lies in the fact that, since sucking is such a great calming device, it's easy to get hooked on sticking a nipple in your kid's mouth every time he fusses. And as you know, babies fuss a lot! After all, it's their only mode of communication. But if you stick something in your baby's mouth every time she voices an opinion, you're setting yourself up for some heavy Jenny Craig bills in the future. So let your baby "talk." It's your job to learn her language, and to feed her only when she's hungry. Don't get me wrong. I'm the first person to say that if you have to take an important call or watch that episode of Oprah's when she gives all the free stuff away, then stick a nipple in your kid's mouth and get to the important things. I'm only saying not to make a habit out of it.

And while we're on the subject of bad things to make a habit out of . . . as your baby grows, and is able to hold his own bottle, you'll be tempted to put him to bed with the bottle—especially at two in the morning when he won't take no for an answer. But don't. If you put your kid to bed with milk or juice, the sugar in it can rot his beautiful budding teeth. There's also a risk of getting an ear infection. If you think it's hard to get your baby to sleep now, wait until an ear infection comes rolling along. Oy vey!

Yes, sticking a nipple in your kid's mouth will send him off to the sandman faster than if he took the autobahn. But unless you want your baby stuck to your chest more than your husband was during your honeymoon, you'll need an alternate form of sucking device that doesn't have the side effect of giving off milk or cause rotting teeth and ear infections. Luckily, there are a couple of options.

A Pacifier

If you're fortunate enough to have a baby who takes a pacifiers (not all of them do. Some spit them out like bad clams), you'll need to have a large supply of them around at all times. You should keep one in your diaper bag, one in your glove compartment, and four thousand in your home. That's because you'll never want to run out of these "suckers." I know that some people are adamantly against pacifiers and give them a bum rap, but I think they're the best thing next to shrimp pot stickers. As long as you don't use them as a cork to plug your kid every time he cries, and keep it there until he's old enough to grow facial hair, I think they're a perfectly acceptable way to calm your baby down.

Which brings me to the biggest binky dilemma. Will your baby get "hooked" on pacifiers? Will he eventually *need* them to calm himself down? Let me ask you this: Who cares? You're so stressed out that your eyebrow hair is falling out. Even if your worst fears come true and your baby does get hooked, you'll deal with it down the road. One night, years from now, the Pacifier Fairy will come and take the pacifier away, leaving a brand-new action figure in its place. (Oh, how I love this fairy. She's the Betty Ford of babyhood addictions. I'm still hoping she'll bring me a shiny new Range Rover to replace my need for slingback sandals.)

A Thumb

If you're lucky, your baby will discover that everything he needs to pacify himself is right at his fingertips. Namely, his thumb (or any finger[s] of his choice). Have you looked at your baby's thumb lately? It's designed to fit just like a nipple. And that's no accident either. Anyone who goes through the miracle of birth will attest to the brilliance of the human body. Everything has its function—except maybe for men's nipples, which serve only as decorations.

Almost every baby sucks a thumb, or some other finger, at some point. Many even do it in the womb. But a true thumb-sucker will generally take to the digit hard by three months purely for comfort and pleasure. We all know there's something to be said for oral gratification. Just ask a cigarette smoker, a nail biter, a pencil chewer, or anyone who eats the whole basket of tortilla chips at a Mexican restaurant before her Margarita arrives.

When it comes to calming devices, thumbs are as convenient as they come. You can't lose it, and your baby can put it in his mouth without any help from you at two in the morning. The downside? I can think of three, possibly even four. It makes their sucking fingernail become as thin as plastic wrap, they may get more colds because they're constantly putting their dirty fingers in their mouths, and, there is no Thumb Fairy to replace their fingers with cherished toys. And

“My daughter still sucks her fingers, and she's in second grade. With her permanent teeth now becoming buck, I wait until after she falls asleep and put a sock on her hand. She wakes up mad at me, but her fingernails are finally normal again so I guess it's working. Unless she wants to pull down two jobs to help pay for her braces, I'm sticking with the plan.”

—Emily

while most kids stop sucking before their permanent teeth come in, there are some who don't. Then you're faced with buck teeth, chewed-up fingers, and big orthodontia bills. Plus, you also have a teenager who hates you because she has to wear braces to the prom because you weren't strong enough to make her stop sucking her thumb when she was a toddler.

Gadgets

If you've visited a baby store or perused one of the hundreds of baby catalogs you now mysteriously receive along with diaper coupons and ads for baby life insurance, then you know about the many gadgets professing to get your tot on the first train to dreamland. Many are bunk, but some actually do help. Just remember to keep receipts of every gadget and gizmo you buy in case it fails. Raising a kid is expensive enough, and you don't want to burn through it all during the first year alone.

The following are a few ideas that tend to get the most positive reviews.

An automatic swing. In the olden days of baby gear (like about ten years ago), you had to wait until your baby was able to sit up before putting her in a swing. But now, along with other life-changing inventions such as self-tanning lotion and caller ID, they created fantastic swings that allow your baby to use them right from the get-go. I can't think of anything more relaxing than rocking in a rhythmic motion, back and forth, back and forth, back and forthhhhhhhhhhhh. Sorry. I dozed off for a sec just thinking about it!

A vibrating chair. We all know that babies love being on top of the washer during the spin cycle. It's one thing you and your baby have in common! But instead of sending him into a sexual frenzy (which is just plain gross), it simply lulls him to sleep. If you put your baby on the washer, make sure that you never leave him unattended. Note: if you haven't been able to face the laundry room because the pile of dirty clothes has grown higher than the Sears Tower, you can buy a bouncy seat with a vibrator built right in.

A white noise machine. These electronic gizmos look similar to radios, but instead of playing music, they calm your baby by offering a wide selection of naturally soothing sounds like "ocean surf" and "rain." The effect can be amazing, although it does make your house sound like a documentary for the Discovery channel. If you don't want to plunk down the big bucks for the thing, just turn on your hair dryer. Your kid will go to sleep, and you can finally make some sense of your hair.

An exercise ball. Who knew that the big, round, plastic sphere that could tone up your body could also tune out your kid? You'll be amazed at how quickly your little one will nod off when you sit down with him in your arms and bounce or rock on the ball. My guess is that the sensation reminds him of the feeling of being in utero, and even at his tender young age, he can still feel nostalgic.

The Life of a Baby Monitor

Speaking of gadgets, a baby monitor is a must. In case you just arrived on our planet, a baby monitor is that miraculous one-way walkie-talkie device that's the first things you set up in the baby's nursery. Sure people never heard of them a mere generation ago, but back then, families didn't live in 3,000-square-foot homes with six bedrooms and three-car garages. Not only is a monitor great when your baby is young, but this incredible piece of baby technology will actually be useful throughout every stage of your child's development, only in several different capacities. Here's a glimpse into its future.

Infancy. Put it on top of your baby's hand-painted dresser and listen for her cries at night.

Toddlerhood. The hand-painted dresser is now painted anew once Petunia found your stash of Sharpie pens. The monitor has been reversed so that the microphone is in your room and the speaker is in hers so that when your kid wakes up for the eighth time that night, you can stay in your warm, cozy bed and say, "Mommy's here, honey. It's okay. Go back to sleep."

Preschool. The monitor has been returned to its original position, but instead of using it at night, you use it during the day when your kid has a playdate to listen to her adorable conversation that makes you smile and fills your heart with joy.

Junior high. Now the monitor is hidden in her room (an easy feat since it's always a pigsty) so you can eavesdrop on her phone conversations to find out what's really going on in her life since she never tells you anything anymore.

High school. The hidden monitor now acts as a form of birth control. Whenever her boyfriend is over, you know the perfect moment to barge into her room, thus preventing her from having to take both poli-sci and Lamaze classes.

Call Security!

A decade from now, you'll spend most of your time steering your adolescent away from addictive substances. But right now, you'll spend most of your time trying to encourage them. When your baby is young and new and has more skin folds than a Shar-Pei, you'll surround her with blankies and stuffed animals in hopes that she'll

❝ My son never seemed interested in anything I'd give him as a security object. Eventually, he found his own: my nursing bra. He carries it with him everywhere and I can't tell you the looks I get from strangers when he caresses it on his face. **❞**

—Veronica

feel comforted and able to fall asleep without any help from bottle or boob.

Not all babies require security objects. Some have the inner strength to just say no. You keep handing them cute chenille teddy bears or pastel-colored blankies, but they have the courage to abstain. On the other hand are babies who are as attracted to security objects as you are to beauty supply stores, and they have no problem getting hooked. The problem, however, is that they get hooked on items that you don't necessarily want them to get hooked on, like a ratty old dishcloth or your husband's smelly tube sock.

If you want a chance at influencing your kid's decision as to what his security item should be, keep the following points in mind:

- Start this project early. Most babies start to attach to objects at three months of age.

- Be sure to limit the size of this object. My daughter fell in love with a giant Po pillow that was bigger than she was. Now, we have to stuff that overgrown alien in our carryon whenever we travel. On the flip side, don't make the security object so small that it'll constantly get lost.
- Keep in mind the durability of the object since it is going to be getting a lot of wear and tear and love over the next few years. Be sure to pick something that you can toss in the washing machine rather than send out to be dry-cleaned.
- Whatever you choose to tempt your child, make sure that it's readily available. You're going to need to get at least three of them if she gets attached (one for the crib, one for the house, and one for the car). If one ever gets lost or ruined, the last thing you'll want to do is spend $500 on eBay for a rare, pre-war stuffed rabbit.

Once your kid finds his security item of choice, look out. Like any other addiction, he'll go through withdrawal symptoms when he's taken off the stuff. He'll cry and scream and steal money out of your wallet to get a fix. Because of this, you must never, and I mean never, be without that security item. Hell hath no fury like a baby without his "nu-nu."

When it comes to washing the security object, be discreet. Don't ever let your kid see you do it or else he'll forever think of you as Mommy Hannibal Lecter. Also, wash it as little as possible. I know that the layers of dirt and drool send your cleaning instinct into overdrive, but think of your kid's security object as your grandma's cast-iron skillet, which has layers of grease and seasonings that you're forbidden to wash away. If you must wash it, do so with unscented soap, or even just plain hot water, and then stick it in a hot clothes drier to kill the dust mites. Kids' noses are very keen, and even April Fresh Downy smells like skunk-ass to your kid when it's on his lovey.

Even if, after all your attempts, your baby chooses that ratty old dishcloth to be his security object, accept it and love it simply because he does. If anything, this'll be good practice for when, years from now, he marries a girl who's overbearing, rude, and a terrible homemaker, and you have no choice but to love her as well. Or at least you let him *think* that you love her, but secretly, have a voodoo doll of her that you keep in your freezer. What? You think your mother-in-law doesn't have one of you?

chapter 5

the zen commandments:
how to get your baby
to sleep through the night

By now, some of you have mastered the art of getting your babies to sleep. After weeks of searching, you've finally found your "it," be it swaddling and a song, a book and a baby massage, or a rendition of *Beauty and the Beast*, including deleted scenes. You're halfway to a good night's rest—because now that you've figured out how to get them to fall asleep at nighttime, you just have to figure out a way to keep them that way.

The first step in the system is to determine if your baby is ready. For that, we turn to our trusty pediatrician and our bounty of baby books. They'll tell you that if your baby is three to four months

old, "generally" he needs to eat only once during the night, if at all. If he's at least ten pounds,
"technically" he should be able to sleep eight hours
without eating, which is eight hours that *you* could
be sleeping as well. And if your baby is six or seven
months old, he "should" be able to sleep through
the night. Because all babies are different, I use
these terms as loosely as the skin on a successful
gastric-bypass patient. But if your baby meets any
of the above criteria and he's waking up more than
he should, you may want to push the issue of sleep.
Unfortunately, this isn't always pretty.

You see, babies, both big and small, wake up
several times during the night. It's a natural part
of the sleep cycle, along with drooling on our pil-
lows and waking up with bed head. When we
big babies wake up, we simply go back to sleep.
But when small babies wake up, they completely
freak out. They don't know where they are, and
more important, they don't know where you are.

That's why, as soon as your baby is physically
ready to sleep through the night, he needs to learn
how to put himself back to sleep when he wakes
up. And he needs to learn how to do this solo,
without the use of nipples or bottles or rocking
or patting, so that when he does wake up in the
middle of the night, he can put himself back to
sleep all by himself.

I know this won't be easy. I realize that life doesn't run as smoothly as new lip liner. You're exhausted, and your baby is already learning so many other important things in life like the intricacies of peekaboo. But whenever you and your baby are ready to take on this challenge, might I suggest the following commandments you can try in hopes of getting your nights back.

COMMANDMENT NUMBER 1:
Make Sure You and Your Partner Are Playing on the Same Team

If you and your mate weren't on sure footing before your baby was born, you're certain to sink in quicksand right about now. That's because nothing chips away at the fragile holes in a relationship more efficiently than sleep deprivation. In the wee hours of the night, when just the sound of your mate's breathing lights a fury in your belly the likes of which no pregnancy heartburn can match, just remember that this is the man you once adored. It's just the tired talking. And tired will drive even the mightiest love to the darkest depths of despair.

The only hope you have of reigniting the passions of your love (okay, to be able to stand being in the same room that he's in) is to get your kid to sleep so that both you and your stud can get some sleep yourselves. Yet, if you both have different opinions as to how this should come about, then attacking this issue is like picking at the already infected scab of your relationship. This should come as no surprise since you've had so many battles since your baby was born, and you're sure to have many more to come. Yes, the stress of having a baby can tear many couples apart. In fact, newborns are the bread and butter of many divorce lawyers.

You both realize that you need to get your kid to sleep through the night. But when it comes to teaching him how, you can't agree on a plan. Your husband can't stomach the idea of letting him cry, and you can't take another sleepless night. He thinks your nurturing gene is weak, and you resent him for not being able to lactate so that he can help out at night. You've come to an impasse and feel that you have nowhere to go but your mother's.

Remember, in most cases, it took the two of you to make this bundle of joy, so don't fall apart now. You and your partner must find a way to get on the same page regarding this, and all future major child-rearing issues. Even if that means *you*, in your completely exhausted state, need to be the bigger person. Dig down deep and find the love that's buried underneath a sink full of dishes and a trash can filled with soggy nipple pads. Take out your photo albums and recall your first date and kiss. Then, when your tummy gets a hint of romantic butterflies, sit down together and discuss how you want to handle your sleeping issues.

I know your husband feels like the enemy, but remember that his world has been turned upside down too. He's no longer the apple of your eye. He's more like the gum underneath your shoe. Now that the baby's born, his needs fall somewhere between cleaning the toilets and pretreating poopy stains. Not only is he exhausted, but he's completely stressed over how he's going to pay for this kid. (Men always worry about the financial part of a kid no matter what tax bracket they're in.) Buried underneath his overflowing inbox and ever-growing pile of bills, he still loves you more than the sun, the moon, and the stars combined.

Lovingly explain that if he's unable to help you in the middle of the night, then he'll need to entertain your methods of getting the baby to sleep—whatever they may be. If he has a different game plan, then *lovingly* make a deal to try one method for a certain time frame, then the other.

"Lovingly" is the operative word here. After all, you can catch more flies with honey than vinegar. And you can catch less grief with your husband if you promise to have sex with him after he agrees to your plan!

Please, if you have strong feelings of discord—okay, disgust—toward your man, don't dismay, and more important, don't divorce. *These feelings will pass as you get more sleep.* Things will settle down, your cells will regenerate, and you will fall in love all over again. You're still in love; you're just too tired to feel it. But one day when you least expect it, you'll gaze at your husband holding your baby or giving her a bath, or better yet, unloading the dishwasher without having been asked, and you'll feel a gut-numbing love for him you never dreamed possible.

COMMANDMENT NUMBER 2:
The Early Bird Catches the Z's

If you're going to teach your kid to fall asleep by himself, do so as early as possible. The younger the child, the more malleable he is. If you think about it, your baby-kins had no trouble falling asleep by himself when he was in utero. He did it all by his little lonesome without the help of a book, a bottle, or a relaxing lavender-scented bath. But somehow, after some time in the outside world, he lost that wonderful ability. He's had weeks, if not months, of living the good life: falling asleep in your comforting arms, being rocked rhythmically in a swing or nursed to sleep. How can he possibly go back to the old days after living the life fantastic?

If your baby is still young, and hasn't moved over to the dark side of sleep despair, keep him on track. Put him down when he's tired, yet still awake, and let him fuss for a bit. Chances are he'll fall asleep in no time. Then you can be one of those couples I hate. You know, the ones who have babies and say they're so easy, they actually forget they're around. You and your partner will sleep well, and your kid will have a house full of siblings.

But if your kid is already hooked on being nursed to sleep or rocked, it may take some work to teach him how to fall asleep on his own again. But it can be done. And it should be done now. Before any more time goes by that allows his desire to turn into a compulsion. For as anyone who's tried to squelch their desire to squeeze blackheads knows, a compulsion is a terrible thing to break.

COMMANDMENT NUMBER 3:
Don't Let Your Baby Sleep Around

When putting your babies to sleep for the night, some of you make the mistake of putting them down in one place and having them wake up in another. For instance, I know many of you still aren't on board with the whole "teaching your kid to fall asleep by himself" thing, so instead, you let him fall asleep in your arms, or a swing, or a vibrating bouncy. Then, once he's out like stone-washed jeans, you transfer him into the crib. When he wakes up in the middle of the night, you're surprised to hear him crying like a baby.

The truth is that you shouldn't be surprised at all. As I said, babies wake up naturally during the night, and I bet you'd freak out too if you went to bed in one place and woke up in another (unless you live with a snorer and are used to waking up on the den sofa). As soon as you're on board about putting your baby to sleep in the same place where he'll wake up, feel free to read on.

COMMANDMENT NUMBER 4:
Don't Get Out of Bed Too Quickly

A strange thing happens to your body after you have a kid, besides getting stretch marks and having your privates not line up the way they did before. You also develop an amazing sense of hearing. You'll find that every little whine and whimper your baby makes in the middle of the night causes you to bolt awake. Then, instead of letting him fuss, you race over to save him because letting him cry is simply too cruel.

What you should know is that if you want to teach your kid to sleep through the night, it's imperative to let him fuss. (By "fuss" I mean let him whimper or cry for a few minutes. This is different than an all-out scream.) This is just what your baby needs to do to fall back to sleep, just as you need to shove your snoring spouse. If you go to your baby the instant he fusses, he'll learn that fussing at night gets him Mommy's loving arms and maybe even a midnight snack.

On that same note, don't be so quick to pull your kid out of bed when he wakes up in the morning. Letting him stay there as long as he's not upset can easily get you another fifteen minutes of sleep. I know that fifteen minutes may not sound like that much, but early-morning sleep is like dog years, and it's worth much more than face value.

COMMANDMENT NUMBER 5:
Engines Run Longer on Full Tanks of Milk

Anyone who's been on a diet knows that it's hard to get a good night's sleep when you go to bed hungry. That's why it's important to stuff your kid like the cavity of a Thanksgiving turkey before you put him down for the night. But sometimes that's much easier said than done.

As you know, babies tend to fall asleep when it's feeding time. This infuriates you since you've calculated that every gulpful of milk equals six minutes of sleep. Falling asleep with a belly half full just won't do. So you wiggle the nipple around in your baby's mouth and do everything you can to wake her up shy of sticking her head in a toilet as your collage roommate did to you after a keg party.

Another obstacle that gets in the way of your baby going to bed with a full belly is that after she eats she tends to barf like a runway model. Now your breasts are empty and your outfit is full of barf. You offer your baby a bottle, but you can't get her to drink anymore. Now, not only

❝My daughter kept waking up a few hours after I put her

down. I tried everything I could to get her to sleep longer,

and I finally realized that I wasn't giving her enough food. As

soon as I doubled the formula in her bottle, she slept through

the night. I decided I'm the worst mom in the world and

don't even deserve to have a houseplant.**❞**

—Kelly

will she be up in a few hours, but you have a full load of laundry to do.

If you do manage to fill up her tank before bedtime and she's still waking up at night, try some of the following ideas:

- Get a few more daytime feedings in. If your kid's caloric needs are being met during the day, she may not be such a snacker at night.
- Top her off at *your* bedtime. This is even better if you're nursing, since breastfeeding ignites hormones that cause you to relax even more than your already exhausted state. Plus, this late-night feeding can be a special time for you and your baby.

There's something romantic about sitting in a rocking chair and nursing your baby, when the rest of the world is asleep. It's moments like this that will tether you to your child with an invisible umbilical cord that's strong enough to weather even the most trying times.

- Stretch out daytime feedings. If your kid's still eating every two hours, gradually stretch it out to three. That way, your baby will be hungrier at feeding time and take in more food, which in turn, will last longer in his belly.

- If you're nursing, get your baby to finish all of the milk in at least one breast. The end of each breast's milk supply is full of something called "hindmilk," which is more rich and filling than the regular stuff. It's the Twinkies cream of breastmilk.

COMMANDMENT NUMBER 6:
The Night Time Is the Right Time for Lull

One vital lesson that you want to convey to your kid is that daytime is the time for play, and nighttime is the time for sleep. That's why when your little enchilada wakes up in the middle of the night, it's important to be as dull as a stewardess giving that preflight safety speech.

If you need to feed your baby, do so while keeping the room dark. Also, think of him as a solar eclipse and avoiding making direct eye contact. Once you see his adorableness, you'll be tempted to sing, play, or give him squishy belly kisses. But don't! Don't even bother changing his diaper unless it's poop-packed or soaking wet. They make diapers so efficient these days they can absorb a kiddie pool. Simply stick a nipple in his mouth and turn the other way. Heck, just pretend he's your husband.

I know this will be a difficult feat, especially when your schnookums looks up at you with his goofy looking grin. (I'm referring to your baby

> **"** I've created a monster. I don't come home from work until after my daughter is asleep, so when she wakes up at about ten and looks at me with her cute face, I take her out of the crib and play with her. Unfortunately, this keeps us both up until after midnight and makes me sleep-deprived all day. I'm just not strong enough to stand up to cute. **"**
>
> —Nadine

now.) You can't believe how much you love this beautiful little creature, and all you want to do is snuggle him and make funny high-pitched oogley-wooogley noises that we grownups tend to do with our young.

Sure, you'll be tempted to look, but turn away, soldier. You're on a mission here, and you've got to be strong. You're dealing with quite a worthy opponent. Personally, I think they must teach a class on parental manipulation in utero since babies are born with a master's degree on the subject. Right now your baby will do anything to seduce you into interaction. *Don't give in.* Even the slightest smile or faintest song is equivalent to giving your kid a handful of NoDoz.

COMMANDMENT NUMBER 7:
No More Midnight Snacks

If your baby is older than six months and still wakes up wanting a home-cooked meal several times a night, chances are it's out of habit rather than hunger. The bad news is that you can blame only yourself for this mess. Okay, you can blame your husband if you'd like, or even your mother if she didn't let you get your ears pierced until after all the other girls did, but chances are it was you who set up this situation. The good news is that you're also the one to get yourself out of it.

I understand how easily you can fall victim to this. After all, how could you possibly deny your child food at night when he's crying for it? He really might be hungry. It's not like babies come with dipsticks in their bellies that measure when they're getting low. Besides, your kid has no concept of night and day. He's used to eating 24/7 so why give it up now? After all, I'm still doing it at my age. But if you want your cutie patooty to sleep through the night, and he's old enough to do so, then the night feedings have got to go. It's that simple. And trust me, if you don't do it now, it'll only get harder when your kid is older and has greater lung capacity.

I know it won't be easy for you. If you're breastfeeding, your boobs will have to go through an adjustment period. They'll be there at 3:00 A.M., ready with a nice warm meal, but you must respectfully decline. Because of this, you'll have to sleep on a couple of large, achy coconuts for a few nights and may even have to deal with night sweats as your hormones adjust to your new milk production schedule. Just sleep on a few towels that you can easily pull off as needed.

It won't be easy for your kid to adjust either. He's used to protesting until he gets his one-course meal. But be strong. Realize that his tears have less to do with hunger and more to do with the fact that he can't fall back to sleep on his own. If you're nursing, send your husband in when the baby cries. Your kid won't be so determined to nurse since he knows that the only thing that's coming out of *his* nipples are a few stray hairs. If you're bottle-feeding, your baby is older than six months of age, and your pediatrician approves, give your baby a bottle of water when he wakes up in the middle of the night. With any luck, he'll think a bottle of H_2O isn't worth all the tears. If you're strong and don't give in, it shouldn't take long for Junior to figure out that the kitchen is closed after lights out.

COMMANDMENT NUMBER 8:
Let Them Eat Cake . . .
or at Least Some Rice Cereal

Who knew that babies could be so controversial? They're basically global warming in infant form. One of the hottest conflicts? At what age should babies start eating solid foods. Everyone has an opinion on the topic, and they're not afraid to voice it. From your mother, to your best friend, to your barista at Starbucks, who really couldn't care less but offers up her advice anyway since she could use a nice tip. Your neighbor swears she started her kids on cereal at two months old, but your sister-in-law is still breastfeeding little Henry, and he's cutting his twelve-year-old molars. Yes, the "right time" to start your kid on solids seems to change as often as fashion trends. "Pink" is the new "black," and "six months" is the new "four months."

When it comes to starting your little precious on solids, there's really only one expert you should turn to: your baby. (Okay, you can consult your pediatrician as well, but your baby really does have a lot to say about the matter.) Does he finish his bottle and still crave more? Is he eyeing your plate with as much desire as you would if Orlando Bloom were lying on it? Since your baby is as unique as a dandruff flake, you have to assess your little one's individual needs and desires.

As of this exact moment in time when I'm sitting at my computer typing these words, the age suggested by pediatricians to start a baby on solids is between four and six months. But, if you're the mother of a kid who's up more than a teenaged boy dreaming of Pamela Anderson, this can seem like an eternity. You fully believe that if you can just add some solid food to your child's diet, especially before bedtime, he'll be able to sleep for a longer stretch of time. Some doctors consider this a myth, so check with your pediatrician, and if she gives you the go-ahead, then by all means, give it a try!

What to feed your little tyke is the next form of controversy. Most people believe you should start on cereals, then add veggies, then fruit, then meat. But there are certain foods that kids are more allergic to—such as strawberries, peanuts, and shrimp—so check with your pediatrician. Again, at this exact moment in time, the first food to start your baby on is rice cereal. But next week it might be vegetables or fruits, or even 2 percent soy lattes if your barista at Starbucks has her way. But then again, she owns stock in the company, so she's a little biased.

COMMANDMENT NUMBER 9:
Just Say No

This ninth commandment isn't just for infants; it can be used for children of all ages. But the point is, if you want your kids to sleep through the night, avoid giving them stimulants or depressants before bedtime. I bet you're saying, "Are you mad? I wouldn't dream of giving drugs to my kid! I'm not like those parents you see on a very special episode of *Oprah*." But the fact is, you could be exposing your child to a slew of anti-sleeping agents without being aware of it. If you don't believe me, here is a list of some potential "drugs" that may be affecting little Petunia's ability to sleep through the night:

Television. Technically, it's not a drug, but it is a stimulant. Sure, watching most children's programs is enough to put *you* to sleep, but they can have the opposite effect on your child. Upbeat music, playful dancing, and colorful sets all stimulate your child rather than lull him to sleep. I know there are actually TV channels and videos especially geared toward infants, but I'd recommend avoiding them when it's close to bedtime.

Alcohol. Some of you may rub dabs of whiskey or bourbon on your babies' gums if they're cutting teeth. You figure with all that crying going on, someone in the house should be buzzed. Although you may think you're helping your baby, *you're not*! Giving alcohol to a baby is incredibly dangerous and can even be fatal. So stop it right here and now because liquor and babies do not mix.

Caffeine. When you think about caffeine, I bet you think of coffee or tea, which I know you wouldn't dream of giving to your kid. But did you know that chocolate and sodas can have caffeine? So can coffee yogurt and coffee ice cream. So be safe and avoid giving your baby anything but breastmilk or formula before bedtime (or cow's milk when he's older than one year).

Sugar. While some doctors say sugar does not hype up kids, I don't think there's any harm to steering clear of sweets, including fruit juices, before bedtime.

Over-the-counter cold medications. When your baby gets a cold, your pediatrician may advise over-the-counter medication. And while it may give some kids relief, it can give moms nothing but misery. That's because not all babies react the same way to medications. Some become drowsy, but others rev up. If you must use an over-the-counter medication, give it a test-drive during the daytime to see if your child gets help or hyper.

COMMANDMENT NUMBER 10:
Force the Issue

You've done all that you can do. You've weaned your baby off nighttime feedings, you've given her rice cereal before bed, and you're as quiet as a gagged monk at nighttime. But still, your baby wakes up at night.

I hate to say it, and I know you hate to hear it, but it may be time to bring in the heavy artillery of teaching your baby how to fall asleep on his own. Up until now, the only lesson your baby has learned is that when he pitches a fit, he's rewarded with his mommy or daddy's loving arms. After all, you've just been going on instinct, and isn't it unthinkable to neglect a crying baby? The answer is yes . . . and no. And in the middle of the night, when your baby is old enough to sleep through the night, the answer is a most definite "no."

If your baby's basic needs are met, then it's time to stop running into his room when he cries. At some point in his life, he has to learn that all the screaming in the world ain't gonna get him a playdate at two in the morning. As soon as he learns this, your baby will stop screaming and everyone will start snoozing. Yes, I know this will be a difficult lesson to teach, but it's better to do it now while your baby is still young, and not capable of slashing your tires for revenge.

When it comes to forcing the issue, you can't help but think of Dr. Richard Ferber who, more than twenty years ago, convinced parents to let their kids cry it out until they were so exhausted, they finally fell asleep. Although this method inspired a critically acclaimed episode of *Mad About You*, it also inspired many tears from freaked-out parents. Now, Dr. Ferber is backpedaling a bit saying that endless crying isn't best for baby, but the concept, and the word "Ferberizing" have already gained worldwide recognition.

When it comes to letting your kid cry it out, you have three avenues to choose from: the "cry it out" method, the "gradual cry it out" method, or the "complete and total wimp out" method. Which to choose? This depends on you, not your baby. Ask yourself how much stress you and your spouse are capable of handling at this point in time. Are you feeling fragile and vulnerable, or are you tired as hell and can't wake up anymore?

With that said, here are a few of the most common, tried-and-true, mother-tested ways of getting your kid to learn how to fall asleep all on his own.

The "Cry It Out" Method

This is by far the most excruciatingly painful, gut wrenchingly horrible, worse-than-childbirth method that you can choose. It's also the most quick and effective. Quite simply, you prepare your offspring for bed when you know he's tired, place him in his crib, kiss him good night, and then leave the room. Here comes the hard part: *You do not go back in.* Your baby will then proceed to scream bloody murder until he falls asleep from sheer exhaustion. This process usually takes a minimum of twenty minutes although it will feel like twenty hours.

The theory behind this cruel and unusual sleeping technique is that when your baby wakes up again in the middle of the night, he won't cry as long. In fact, each time your baby wakes up, he should cry less and less until he finally learns that there's no point in crying because you won't come in to rescue him. Little does your baby know that you and your husband are in the next room quietly killing each other while the neighbors have called the police to investigate child abuse, and your older child has run away to live with the barren couple down the street. But then, just when you thought you couldn't take it one more minute and you've officially lost five years of your lifespan, your baby stops crying!

If you decide upon this method of self-destruction, shore yourself up. Surround yourself with plenty of dark chocolate and apple martinis. Warn the neighbors, send your older child to stay with Grandma, and install a bolt lock on that nursery door. And when you can't take your baby's screams for even one more second, use your Lamaze breathing. It didn't do a hell of a lot of good for childbirth, but it may ease the pain now.

Be warned. When you listen to your baby's cries, you'll start to second-guess yourself. You'll wonder how something that feels so wrong could be so right. How do the experts know that your baby won't suffer a lifetime of insecurities because you weren't there for her when she cried out? Will this experience cause future night terrors, sleeping disorders, and a steady stream of loser boyfriends all because she'll be too afraid to be by herself?

You may also fear that she's in physical harm. What if she rolled over and cut her lip? What if she threw up all over herself? It's horrific not being able to check on her, which is why God invented video monitors. Yes, they can be pricey, but you can go in on one with other mommies and share it when it's their turn to force the sleeping issue.

Realize that the first night will be the worst and by far the most difficult. Each episode after that should be a bit easier and take less time. And about it being traumatic? Not as much as you think. Babies, like dogs, have no concept of time. They don't know if they've been upset for five minutes or fifty. It'll be years before they can read a clock, decades if it's not a digital. I'll guarantee that in the morning, your little love bug won't remember a thing and will still greet you with that same beautiful smile she always does.

But while the experience may not be traumatic for your baby, you can count on it being *very* traumatic on your marriage. While your kid is freaking out, you'll never hate your spouse more. Either he'll want to go in and save his kid, in which case you'll think he's weak, or he'll forbid you from going in to save her, in which case you'll think he's evil. It's a lose-lose situation. But as they say for all bad things, and when your dog swallows your wedding ring, this too shall pass.

The "Gradual Cry It Out" Method

If you find that going cold turkey is a "fowl" way to make your kid learn how to fall asleep, then this second method may be a better way to go. As before, prepare your little sweet cheeks for bed when you know he's tired, place him in his crib, and then skedaddle out of the room. Next, you and your partner wait a predetermined amount of time before going back in. This time frame is one that both of you agree to beforehand and is based on how long you think you can bear to hear your innocent schnookums cry without running in to save him. It can be as little as a few minutes or up to an hour if you have the strength of one of those guys who can walk on hot coals.

Let's say for this example you decide upon ten minutes. You say good night, leave the nursery, and synchronize your watches. Then you spend the next ten minutes sobbing, fighting, having heart palpitations, and praying to the Lord above that your sweet baby doll will fall asleep. After ten eternal minutes, the clouds part, a chorus of angels burst into joyful song, and you're finally allowed to go back into the room. You rush to your tear-stained tot and reassure him that you haven't boarded a flight to Bora Bora. "Mommy and Daddy are here. We love you! We love you!" You can pat your baby gently and whisper reassuring words, but whatever you do, *do not pick up your baby*. If you do, you will go directly to jail and be sentenced to eighteen years of living with a kid who can never sleep through the night. Sorry, but these are the rules.

After a few tender moments, you say good night again, leave the room, and claw at the nursery room door until you have nothing left but bloody stumps where your fingers used to be. This time, your baby is allowed to cry for *eleven* minutes. Afterward, you burst into the room again. "Mommy and Daddy are here. We

love you! We love you!" The next time the crying period is twelve minutes. Then thirteen. And
so on and so on until either your stubborn child
finally falls to sleep, or you and your mate col-
lapse from exhaustion.

Although some babies do well under this plan,
others do not. They see your appearance at their
bedsides as fuel to stoke their already enraged
flames. "Why aren't you picking me up like you
always do? Quit patting me already and get me
out of this f*&%ing crib!! And what the heck
are you saying to me anyway? I don't know what
you're saying!! I'm screaming here and you're just
standing there whispering and patting!!!"

Even with the downfalls, the "gradual cry it
out" method is certainly worth a try. The worst
things that can happen are that your kid doesn't
fall asleep by himself and you have to regrow
your fingernails. But if this method still sounds
like more than you can bear, I have one more idea
I'll throw your way . . .

The "Complete and Total Wimp Out" Method

For those of you who are total basket cases
when your babies cry, and whose spines are as
firm as cherry Jell-O, this is the plan for you!
This tried-and-true method is one where you put
your baby to bed in her crib when you know she's

tired, turn off the lights, and then sit in the dark with her and talk to her from across the room if she fusses. "Mommy is here. Mommy loves you." The method behind this madness is that your baby will feel secure just knowing that you're in her presence, then blissfully drift off to sleep.

I'm not joking. This is an actual method for putting your baby to sleep. Just the thought of it makes me laugh. I doubt if it would've worked on my kid's dolls let alone my kid, but neverthe-less, people swear by it. Somebody always knows somebody whom it worked for, but personally, I've never actually met that "somebody." They must live off in a far-away land where crime doesn't exist, health care is free, diet food tastes good, and babies always sleep through the night.

Yes, I know there are some of you who think that even this method will be too stressful. You can't bear to sit helpless when your baby cries, and you know you'll be pulling him out of his crib faster than a pint of cookies and cream on the day you get your period. So if you lack the fortitude to try this method, turn to the man you promised to love, cherish, and pick up after till death do you part. Send your husband in the baby's room to comfort your baby. Sure, there's a good chance you'll find him conked out next to the crib, which will only set up another bad habit. But then again, husband and baby asleep in the next room while you sleep alone in your great big bed. Hmmmm. This may be the most brilliant idea in the history of child psychology.

Disclaimer

Sadly for some, even the most drastic methods of "assistance" don't produce sleep in their babies. If you've tried your devil-dog best to help your kid sleep through the night and he still doesn't do it, consult your pediatrician. You might be dealing with an illness, allergy, or alien, and you don't want to take any chances. If your doctor says that Junior is as perfect as David Beckham's abs, take comfort in the fact that this *will* pass. Eventually, your baby will be old enough to entertain himself

> **We let our daughter cry it out for three nights straight and then called in a 'baby sleep expert.' After hearing our daughter's endless cries, even she broke down and went running into the nursery. She said, 'I've never seen a baby cry this much. I can't take it any more. That will be two hundred dollars please.'**
>
> —Katie

in the wee hours of the night—even if it means hanging out at the arcade with his buds doing God knows what. But as long as you're sleeping, you probably won't care either.

chapter 6

i scream! you scream!
we all scream for naptime!

You bring your baby home from the hospital and wonder, "Does this thing ever stop sleeping?" Fast-forward a few weeks and you're thinking, "Does this thing ever sleep?" True, for the first few weeks, most of your little peanut's day is spent in the Land of Nod, but gradually a pattern develops where he sleeps more at night, and less during the day. Then, around the age of three months, the day sleeping develops into two nap periods, and you officially become the parent of a napper.

As you're already aware, because you neurotically compare every aspect of your baby to other
babies his age (yes, we all do it and we'll never stop
no matter how old our kids get) all babies are different. And that's true for how a baby naps as well.
Some fall asleep quickly while others need to cry
it out a bit. Some can only nap in their cribs while
others sleep around more than a young Elvis Pre-
sley. Since you can't always get your baby to nap
where you want, when you want, for as long as you
want, you can be sure that there will be some uni-
versal frustrations. On that note, let's delve into
the wonderful and willful world of naps that begin
at infancy and last throughout toddlerhood.

The Anatomy of a Nap

A dictionary defines a nap as a set period of time
during the day when a baby rests and regener-
ates. A mommy defines it as a set period of time
that she has to do all the stuff she can't get done
when the baby is awake. Yes, when your baby is
napping, it's your time to pay the bills, cook the
meals, return the phone calls, clean the house,
take a shower (if you're really lucky), and buy
all the gifts for your husband's side of the family
that are somehow now your responsibility to take

care of. Sure, the baby books may tell you that when your kid naps, you should nap too, but as you know, some things are much easier read than done.

The simple act of taking a nap can be quite a complicated endeavor. That's because there are so many questions that surround the subject. "How long should a nap be?" "How do I know when my kid is ready for his nap?" And, "How am I possibly going to get everything done in that short amount of time?" Since you have more questions than when you first laid eyes on your electric breast pump, let's go through them one by one.

To answer your first question about how many naps he needs, find out how long a baby his age needs to sleep, then subtract the amount of hours he sleeps at night, and the remainder is how long he should sleep during his naps. In order to find out how much sleep he needs, find a baby sleeping chart (there's one on page 53). But you should pay as much attention to them as you do the red curb at the "loading and unloading" section of the airport. All babies are different and can vary from the norm. Besides, they can't read yet and therefore don't always know what's best for them.

Second, how will you know when your kid is ready to take his nap? Look for the same signs as you would at bedtime: a yawn, an eye rub, or general fatigue (no, not your fatigue since that's ever-present). You should also look for signs that are less apparent such as general crankiness, or a kid who's quieter and less animated than usual. It always feels as if you're walking a tightrope when deciding upon naptime. If you put your baby down too early, he won't be tired enough to fall asleep. If you put him down too late, he could be overtired and therefore too tired to fall asleep. (See "Past the Point of No Return" on page 46.) That's why, as soon as your kid shows the signs of fatigue, get him to bed ASAP! Everyone out of the way! Clear the roads! Coming through! God

❝ Whenever I put my daughter down for a nap, I'd try to take a nap myself. But I'm so stressed out thinking about everything that has to get done that I can't fall asleep. Plus, I'd keep looking at the clock and counting down the minutes until she's due to wake up, and found the pressure to be way too much to take! **❞**

—Janie

save the soul who comes between a mommy and a baby who is ready to nod off to naptime.

"But what if I put my baby down for his nap and he cries?" To that I say, if he cries a bit, let him cry. He might need to fuss to put himself to sleep, just like at night. He can't simply read a few chapters of the latest Danielle Steel novel and flick off the lights. You can pat or rub his back if you must, but resist taking him out of the crib unless he gets hysterical. If he passes the fussy stage, travels deep into hysterical and doesn't calm down after a few minutes, there's not much you can do but take him out of the crib and try again a bit later. If he does get hysterical, chances are he's overtired and you may need to get out the big guns of driving him around or putting him in a swing to get him down. But like any other addictive substance, don't get in the habit of it.

"But what if my baby and I aren't home during naptime?" That's a good question and leads me to my next napping point: flexibility. Not everyone has the luxury of being home twice a day for a one- to three-hour chunk of time. I know that many a nap will be spent in cars running errands or in strollers during their older sisters' ballet classes. I'm just saying, in the best-case scenario, you should put your child down for regular naps in his own crib, where he'll sleep better, deeper, and longer than he would on the go.

And while we're on the best case scenarios, it's also best to let your kid fall asleep by himself, just like at nighttime. If you can get him to do this, he can also do it when he wakes up in the middle of the night, and when you're on date night and a babysitter has to put him to bed, or when you're at work and he's at day care, and on and on it goes. If you don't teach him this important lesson now, you could be faced with a phone call on his wedding night asking you to sing a round of "Twinkle, Twinkle, Little Star" so he can finally get some shuteye.

Oh, and about that burning question about how you can possibly do all the things that need to get done during his nap? Simply put, you can't. So don't even try. Accept the fact that you won't have all your errands run and have sparkling clean floors until your kid is out of the house. But you don't have to accept the fact that your husband can't pick out a gift for his own brother. It's not fair that you have to do everything!

Car Trouble

It's one o'clock in the afternoon and you're cruising home from Mommy and Me, brooding over the fact that all the other babies can sit up while yours keeps falling over like a sock puppet. You glance in your rearview mirror and notice that your little sock puppet is starting to nod off. Holy crap! He's not due to take his nap for another thirty minutes! In fact, you've timed it out just perfectly so that you'll be home in time to put him down for his two-hour afternoon nap! Panicked, you blast the air-conditioning and belt out an operatic version of "Itsy Bitsy Spider." But it's no use. He's out cold.

Yes, as frustrating as it is, falling asleep in the car before naptime is as common as buying a size seven shoe even though you know your feet have spread to a size eight. And, like that small shoe, your kid falling asleep in the car can make you miserable. For once your child falls asleep, there's not a thing you can do about it. Go ahead and try. Open all the windows. Reach around and tickle his feet. Nothing is going to work.

Now that you've pulled in the driveway with a conked-out kid, what can you do? Sure, you could wake him up, but that could have two horrific outcomes. One, he could have the demeanor of a disgruntled postal worker, or, two, he could count that five-minute doze as a power nap and be up until bedtime.

So what's the solution? There really is only one. *Do not* drive any farther than five minutes from your house until you child reaches the age of twelve. Short of that, you're faced with two things:

Let Your Baby Sleep in the Car

For those of you who are conjuring up images seen on the evening news, hear me out. I'm not saying that you should leave your kid at the mall parking lot in an unattended vehicle on a blazing hot day summer's day while you shop for new bras. What I'm saying is to let your baby sleep in a comfortable, shady, safe location, with the windows open and the birds singing in the blue sky above, and you hovering within eyesight.

If you plan it right, you can even turn this problem into productivity. You'd be surprised at how many things you can accomplish while your kid drools away in the backseat. Think of your side door as a mobile desk and fill it with magazines or catalogs that you've wanted to go through. You can also keep your checkbook and some bills in there to catch up on your bookkeeping. If you have a cell phone, now's a great time to catch up on phone calls like the one to your insurance company to get them to pay for all the baby crap you swiped from the hospital. With all this stuff in your car, you may actually look forward to her dozing off in transit.

The only downside to having your kid nap in the car is that she may not sleep as long as she would in her crib, especially if the car engine is turned off. Sure, you can keep it running, but that's bad on the environment as well as bad on your wallet. If you know already that your kid isn't a good car sleeper, you can always resort to plan B:

The Car to House Transfer (CTHT)

Don't panic. It's not as scary as you think. You just have to go through a trial-and-error period to see which method works best for you and your baby. The goal is to get your sleeping kid out of the car and into the house without waking him up. Here are some different "car-to-house" transfer techniques that you can try.

"Baby in Car Seat" Transfer

Remove the *entire* car seat from your car. As you remove the baby from the car, shade his eyes from the strong sun rays, which can startle him awake. Then carry him into the house. Place the car seat on the floor of the nursery, or wherever you want your baby to nap. If your baby is a light sleeper, roll up a towel or receiving blanket and place it under the front end of the car seat so that your baby rests in a more inclined position.

"Stroller as Interim Mechanism" Transfer

Gently lift your sleeping kid out of the car seat and quickly place her in a stroller. Immediately rock your baby back and forth to continue the sensation of the car movement. If your baby wakes up a bit, she will probably go back to sleep at this point. Stroll your baby into the house, being sure to keep a slow rocking movement. Gently stop moving and make a pact with God that if your baby stays asleep, you'll switch to the Earth-friendly plant fertilizer even though it doesn't make your garden as lush as the chemical kind.

"Contort Body into Shape of Car Seat" Transfer

(Note: This move works best as a "car to couch" transfer, as the "mid-day arms to crib baby drop" isn't as successful—even with the pros.) Lean over your baby in the car. Gingerly unhook the seat belt (think bomb squad here).

Cover your baby's body with your own, then lift him out of the car seat, maintaining the car seat's body shape. Carry your baby into the house and gently lower him onto the couch. Push a chair up against the couch so that there is no risk of him falling off.

A Lose-Lose Situation

It's five thirty in the evening. Your baby is in the den playing with an educational toy, listening to classical music. You're in the kitchen preparing an organic, health-conscious gourmet meal for your family while watching *Nova* on PBS. Okay, okay. . . . Your baby is zoning out in front of *Teletubbies* while you're in the kitchen nuking some neon-colored macaroni and cheese while watching *E! True Hollywood Story*. Regardless of the scenario, your baby nods off in mid-tubbie custard.

Again, the problem remains, what are you supposed to do now? Wake him up and deal with a cranky baby until his bedtime, or let him sleep straight through dinner and run the risk of having him wake up at four in the morning hungry and raring to go for the day?

Many "experts" would advise that you wake up your child and put him to bed at his regular bedtime. But then again, these "experts" aren't the ones who'll have to deal with him for the next three hours. Besides, they're the ones who said things like drinking coffee will stunt your growth and you'll catch cold if you go outside with wet hair, so what the hell do they know? These "experts" would also be adverse to your choice of dinner and, even worse, frown on you for letting your kid watch TV at all. Great, thanks for the advice, Now let's talk reality.

In real life, we moms tend to deal with situations like this on a case-by-case basis. For instance, if little Petunia falls asleep right before dinner, and you've had such a horrible day that you're one step away from shaving your head and joining a cult that frowns upon things like procreation, then by all means take the night off and go to bed early. Sure, you may be up at 4:00 A.M., but at least you'll still have hair.

If, on the other hand, it's your *kid* who's had the bad day and you're feeling strong, then by all means wake him up. Sure, he'll be pissed off, but he'll get over it. He's going to have many occasions to be mad at you throughout his lifetime like when you kiss him goodbye in front of his friends, or when you refuse to buy him those trendy sneakers that all the other kids have because they cost more than your new hotel-style sheets from Pottery Barn that you simply couldn't resist.

Keep in mind, this "not sure whether to wake your kid up or not" also applies to a nap that lasts much longer than usual. While it's great to have a chunk of time during the day when you don't have to deal with things like diaper changes and projectile vomiting, you also stress out knowing that your baby won't go to bed until midnight because he won't be tired. How could he be after a four-hour nap? You do the math.

And while this to-wake-or-not-to-wake confusion is horribly difficult to deal with, there are some things in life that are even worse. So, in hopes of putting this naptime frustration in perspective, here are a few worse things that could happen in life than having to deal with a messed-up sleeping schedule:

- Your husband tells you he's leaving you because he found his soul mate in Tori Spelling.
- Your older child hands you an empty container of birth control pills and tells you that she just ate some candy.

- You lock your keys, and your baby, inside the car.
- Your computer crashes along with the thing you use to back up the files.
- You weigh yourself and discover that you somehow found the ten pounds that you've managed to lose.
- You slip your feet into your favorite pair of pumps and instantly realize why your closet has smelled like poop for the past few days.
- Since nothing else has worked, you try to remove the sap from your car hood with nail polish remover, but don't figure out the problem with this strategy until it's too late.
- Your husband's company informs him that, instead of his annual, much-needed Christmas bonus, they've decided to make a generous donation in his name instead.
- Your period's late!

Catnaps Make You Dog-Tired

Sometimes it happens. You give birth to a baby who doesn't require as much sleep as other babies. Especially during the day. While your stay-at-home mom friends are bragging about their kids' three-hour naps, during which time they exercise and have magnificently rewarding at-home careers, your baby blinks for an extended period of time and wakes up feeling refreshed. If you're a stay-at-home mom yourself, these catnaps will leave you dog-tired.

Let's face it. All mommies live for their babies' naps. It's the chunk of time that they can get things done and be productive. (Okay, so we watch reruns of *Sex and the City*, but let's keep that to ourselves.) It's when we can finally take a break from our constantly needy child and take some time for ourselves. Without this crucial downtime period each day, we would build up as much tension as an inmate before a conjugal visit.

While most babies take long naps for an hour or more at a stretch, many of them do not. If your baby isn't one of the "most," you can feel gypped. It's not fair that other moms are spending hours surfing the Web and checking out the celebrity gossip sites while you barely have time to make instant oatmeal. If your baby wakes up from his nap sooner than you'd like, there are a few things you can try to do to get him to sleep longer.

For one thing, don't put your child down for his nap when you know it's close to feeding time. A full and happy tummy is one that will sleep longer and won't wake up due to hunger. You should avoid loud, sharp noises. (Personally, I think everyday noises are fine and should be encouraged since your baby needs to live in the real world.) Set the phone on "low" and put a sign up on your door that says "please knock." Also, be sure to cover up your baby so that he stays warm, but not too warm. A kid who's too hot or too cold won't sleep as long as one who's just right. And finally, make sure that your baby's clothing is comfortable and that she's not sleeping on any hard buckles or hair ties. I know that most of these tips are quite obvious, but haven't we all hired electricians to fix broken television sets that simply weren't plugged in?

If you've tried all these tips and your kid is still taking short naps, well, then I guess you're just plain screwed. Like anything else in your life that you can't control, you have no choice but to accept it, or better yet, rationalize it. Tell yourself that these short naps mean that your kid will be smarter because he'll have more time to learn. After all, I've heard it said that Martha Stewart needs only four hours of sleep a night, and she turned out okay—well, maybe a bit neurotic about painting the handles of her garden tools in eggshell colors, but you get my drift. We women are great at rationalizing, which explains why we have stuff like that expensive hotel bedding from Pottery Barn in the first place.

He Ain't Heavy, He's My Brother . . . Making Noise and Waking Me Up from My Nap!

Tempting as it may be, we're not going to discuss sibling rivalry at this juncture. This is a book about sleep. And interestingly enough, napping can produce issues far more heinous than any Cain and Abel scenario. More specifically, I'm talking about the difficulties of having your baby take a nap while his older sibling is not napping. Instead, this older sibling is running around the house with a towel wrapped around his neck for a cape and is busy saving the world. You've begged and pleaded and told him over and over again to be quiet while the baby's sleeping, but he simply refuses. The way he sees it, it's *your* fault for bringing this bothersome creature home in the first place, and the most that he's going to do for you is not drop-kick it out the front door.

Besides, there's nothing fun for a four-year-old to do that involves being quiet and sensitive to the fact that a baby is sleeping. They can't yell. They can't pound. And they definitely can't do their most favorite-est thing in the world:

have a playdate. That's because the only thing that's more stimulating to your baby than his older sibling is his older sibling's friend. And the only thing that's harder to keep quiet than your kid is someone else's kid. Put these two factors together, and you have the makings for a baby who won't nap, a house that's out of control, and yet another reason to shave your head and join that cult.

If this is the woe that you're facing, I offer you the Holy Grail of the baby-napping-with-an-older-sibling-around-the-house dilemma: the one-child household. Generally, parents with just one kid are more than happy to have your kid come over to play at their houses. Since there are no siblings for their only children to ~~torment~~ play with, the parents spend most of their days playing dollies and trucks with them and are bored out of their cotton-pickin' gourds. They would like nothing more than your four-year-old to come over and take over the role of "playmate."

Thankfully, more and more people are deciding to have just one child so I urge you to mine this resource. Set up playdates for your older child during your baby's naptime. Then you can reciprocate by telling the other parents that you'll have their children over one day soon. Of course, you'll just tell them this, but in fact, you never will. What, are you crazy? You have enough havoc at your house without throwing another kid in the mix!

Shy of that, there are a few more tricks of the trade you can try. When the little one naps, keep the older ones quiet by:

Spending some much-needed one-on-one time with them. But do so outside! Plant a garden, play with the hose, collect worms (or for those of you with weak stomachs, collect rocks instead).

Playing a computer game. No matter how young your child, there's a computer game to match their interest. Plus, they sell a computer mouse that's kid friendly and far less frustrating for their tiny fingers to use.

Playing the quiet game. Both you and your kid must whisper during naptime and your child is rewarded by stickers or treasures. Remember to reward your child for being quiet instead of punishing him for being loud. It'll only build up more resentment toward his younger sibling, which, as you've learned last week when he packed his baby brother in a suitcase and put him outside, there's plenty of already!

chapter 7

setbacks and complications

You've finally got your baby on a beautiful schedule. He naps on cue, goes to bed at a decent hour, and wakes up with a sunny disposition after a good night's sleep. You and your man clink your champagne glasses and let out a long, luxurious sigh of relief, "Whew, we did it. We're finally the parents of a perfect sleeper!" Great. I'll give you a few moments to savor the moment and enjoy your false sense of permanence. Humm de dumm dumm dumm.

Okay, time's up. Here comes your reality check: The only thing you can count with a baby is—nothing! Everything you know is going to change, again and again and again. Once you accept *that* reality, then can appreciate the

good times, because you know that they're as
fleeting as having no laundry in the hamper.

As soon as you give up any expectations as to
what a parenting experience should be like, then,
and only then, will you not be disappointed. For
the reality is that having a baby is far more difficult than it's portrayed on any TV show like
The Brady Bunch, *Full House*, or *Beverly Hills,
90210*. (Okay, so technically they weren't babies,
but they certainly acted like it.)

Having said that, if your kid continues to
sleep like an angel, congratulations and enjoy the
fun while it lasts. Life has a way of evening things
out in the end, and you're sure to get yours during
the turbulent teenage years when your kid develops a fondness for body piercing. For the rest of
you, enjoy your delusion of stability because you
can count on certainties like death, taxes, and any
one of the following things to happen to make all
the perfect sleeping habits go away.

Cry Baby

You made it through the pregnancy, the episiotomy, and the stress of figuring out how to set up
that damn infant car seat. You bring your beautiful bundle home from the hospital and are in com-

plete and total bliss (except of course when you sit down on a hard chair . . . ouch!). You stare at your baby who's happy and content in her crib.

And then it happens. That whimper. That whimper that turns into a whine. That whimper that turns into a whine that slips into a cry. That whimper that turns into a whine that slips into a cry, and then escalates into the most blood-curdling wail imaginable! You feed her, burp her, change her, and rock her, but nothing softens the brain-numbing timbre of your baby's screams. Dear Lord, a dingo just ate your baby and left this crying thing in its place!

Then suddenly, just as mysteriously as it starts, it stops. Silence has returned to your world, and your bundle of joy is back, cooing, drooling, sleeping, and sucking. In other words, utter perfection. That is until the next night, and the night after that, and the night after that, when the blood-curdling wail returns with Swiss-timing accuracy.

I hate to be the one to break it to you my friend, but I fear that you might be looking at the dreaded C word: colic. The ugliest word in all of mommy-dom. It's the biggest sleep-killing, dream-busting, divorce-inspiring condition that can plague a new parent. And there is no escape from the dark abyss that is now your world. At least not for the next few months.

Just as all babies are as unique as cheese puffs, colic can manifest itself in many different ways. Having said that, there are some tried-and-true signs that indicate that your child's crying jags are more than just plain old infant PMS:

- At around three weeks of age, your previously cheerful cherub begins to cry inconsolably. This crying jag often begins in the late afternoon and can last well into the wee hours of the night. Although it does tend to appear in the evening, this "unhappy" hour can come at any time of day.

- The cry isn't like the others that can simply be appeased by cuddling or cuisine. Desperate, you search for anything that can explain your baby's shrieks, such as an eyelash in her eye, a minuscule hangnail, or shards of glass in her diaper. But unfortunately, you find nothing.

- Your baby becomes active and agitated, clenches her fists, pulls her knees to her chest, then kicks them out again as if in pain. You pray for a tiny fart or a poop, but even if they come, they do not spell relief.

- Your baby seems hungry and is rooting madly. You shove a nipple in her mouth and with great relief, she starts to suck. But only for a few seconds. Then, she spits it out and starts crying and rooting again.
- You assess your breastmilk supply: Yes, it's there. If you're on formula, you rush to the store and change to another brand. Still no luck.
- You put your kid in the car and drive around (the strongest sleep-evoking method you can try without a prescription). But still, she does not stop crying.

Do not panic! You will get through this. Colic is a fairly common mystery ailment that visits some 20 percent of all babies, and there are some ways to deal with it. To begin with, try some of the comfort methods listed in Chapter 2. Next, check out one of the truckloads full of support groups, Web sites, and books offering up oodles of crazy remedies. Bottom line, colic is not a chronic condition, and in three to six months, it *will* pass.

During this difficult time, focus on the positive. The good news is that it's believed babies who have colic as infants grow up to be extremely successful human beings. But then again, it's also believed that if your left breast was bigger during pregnancy, you should have had a girl. I don't know if any of that is true, but I do know one important fact. If your marriage can survive colic, then other things like infidelity, bankruptcy, and finding your husband dressed in ladies' underwear won't seem like such big obstacles to overcome!

Under the Weather and Out of Your Mind

When your baby gets sick, you get sick too. That's because all your hard work and marital stress of teaching your kid to sleep through the night gets tossed out the window . . . along with your sanity. Understandably, it's hard for your baby to sleep at night when he's not feeling well and is years away from taking good sleeping aids like NyQuil or a hot toddy.

When your child is sick, you can forget about making him "cry it out" or fuss for a while in

" The only time my energetic, on-the-go kid wants to cuddle is when he's sick. I'm tempted to forgo his yearly flu shot just so I can get in some good snuggle time. "

—Anonymous mom

his crib. Most of us compassionate mammas don't
even make our sick babies sleep in their cribs at
all. Instead, we let them sleep anywhere they
want—be it in our cars, in our beds, or at the
Ritz-Carlton. Let's face it, when our kids are sick,
our maternal instincts kick into overdrive, and
we'll do anything to turn our babies' red cheeks
back to rosy pink.

There are plenty of home remedies and
homeopathic ways to help your child feel better
when he's sick. But if you're looking for some
more powerful remedies, give your pediatrician
a call. He'll probably recommend baby Tylenol,
Motrin, or any other mild over-the-counter medications that are specifically made for children
to help lower their fevers or dry up their stuffy
noses. While you're on the phone with the doc,
get the correct dosage and make sure you buy the
right formula. As you'll notice on the drug store
shelf, pain reliever can be labeled as "infant,"
"child," or "junior." Again I must caution that
if you venture into the land of pharmaceuticals,
give it a test-drive during the daylight hours. If
you don't, be prepared for a baby who is sick, *and*
up all night as well.

Although in most cases these drugs do help
your baby feel better, they can also bring on
the unexpected the first time you try them out.

Yes, giving a baby medicine is like a weekend in Vegas: Anything can happen. The label says it may cause drowsiness, but your kid gets as amped up as Richard Simmons. Or it warns you about hyperactivity, but your little bambino is passed out on the kitchen floor alongside your Labrador retriever. In time, you'll get to know how your child will respond to medications.

If your baby's suffering from a cold and has a stuffed-up nose, you should keep his head elevated so that it can drain. Place a book or a blanket underneath the head of the crib mattress. If your baby's young enough, he may fare better sleeping in his car seat.

If your child's suffering with a stomach virus, then you have my most sincere condolences. Not only will a child with the stomach flu emit so many bodily fluids that your house will resemble a crime scene, but he'll do so without any warning what-so-ever. If you decide to have your baby sleep with you, cover your sheets with hazmat gear . . . or at least a few towels. It's much easier to remove a towel than to strip a whole bed at three in the morning.

If you do take your baby out of his crib when he's sick, stick him right back in there as soon as he's on the mend. Of course there'll be some resistance and he may protest loud and clear. But be strong and be persistent. Within a few days, you'll come down with whatever illness your kid was sporting and you'll need to get a decent night's sleep!

The Shot Heard Round the Night

Although you can count on your pediatrician to placate your fears about strange rashes and odd-shaped poops, you can also count on him to screw up your kid's pristine sleeping habits. That's because every time he gives your kid a vaccination, you need to have a shot as well . . . a shot of tequila that is, in order to deal with the potential side effects that come along with vaccinations.

Don't get me wrong, I appreciate vaccines. In fact, I am in awe of them. God bless Jenner, Salk, and all those other brilliant thinkers who came up with the miracles of science that protect our offspring from pain. They've saved the world from more suffering than the guy who canceled *Joey.*

After your pediatrician gives Junior his vaccination, he may experience some tenderness at the site of injection, and even have a small fever later on. Some moms believe that immunizations also cause their kids to have diarrhea or runny noses.

Others say it makes them fussy, or even drowsy. Still others blame them for their fender benders and overdrawn checking accounts. It's always easier to point the blame anywhere but yourself.

If your child does get some ouchies due to a vaccine, ask your pediatrician about relieving the discomfort with a mild pain reliever before putting him down to bed that night. Not only will it help him sleep through the night, but it'll help him from having to learn how to fall asleep by himself again, and not in his mother's loving arms. As you know, a kid can become addicted to being held faster than you can become addicted to Cinnabons at the mall. Ah, if only these great thinkers of science can come up with a vaccine for those warm, delicious things!

Molars, Incisors, Bicuspids, Oh Crap!

If the Tooth Fairy is responsible for taking those adorable little white nuggets away and leaving dollar bills in their place, then the Teething Goblin is most certainly the one who rams these little suckers in to begin with, leaving only a miserable baby and sleepless nights in his wake.

While baby teeth arrive in approximately the same order, their arrival times can vary. Babies can get teeth as early as three months or as late as a year. But normally, you can count on your baby's first tooth to arrive the exact day that you've finally taught her how to sleep through the night.

Keep in mind, not all babies have teething problems with the same severity. Some, the ones who will grow up and not need epidurals to give birth, will show no signs of cutting teeth at all. One day they'll simply smile at you, and you'll notice new pearly whites in their gums. But many other babies will be miserable for days on end until the teeth finally cut through.

Here are a couple of points to know about cutting teeth. One, certain teeth may be more problematic to cut than others. Just because your child didn't shed a tear with one tooth doesn't mean she won't cry a river of tears with another. My daughter had the worst time with the upper pointy ones. It was as if she were cutting steak knives. Two, I found that it was always darkest before the dawn of a new tooth, so you can expect the pain, and therefore the fussiness, to be the most intense right before the tooth finally makes an appearance.

During the day, you can ease the pain with a teether, which is a plastic, safety approved, chew toy for infants. Keep some in the fridge since the cold tends to numb the pain. If you don't have any teethers, dampen a clean washcloth with some ice water and give it to her to suck on. If you don't have clean washcloths, crush up some ice and tie it up in one of your baby's clean socks and let her suck on it. If you don't have any washcloths or clean socks, well then, looks like you have some laundry to do.

As bad as the daytime is to deal with, it's the nighttime that's the worst for teething pain (as well as head colds and bad breakups). Sure, you can use the holistic cures, numbing gels, or even Tylenol if your pediatrician allows, but don't expect them to work miracles. They're usually effective only for a few hours, so your kid may have a problem sleeping through the night.

If she does wake up, it's your call as to whether to take your fussy baby out of her crib. If you're sure her cries are due to teething (which is a pretty safe bet when she's covered in drool and gnawing little totem poles onto her crib slats), you may want to consider leaving her inside. There's gonna be a lot of teeth a comin' over the next few years. If she gets inconsolable, I know you'll be tempted to nurse her back to sleep, but with those new razor-sharp teeth coming in, this may mark the end of your nursing days!

I'm Bitchin' to Travel

When it comes to traveling with a baby, I've got three words of advice for you . . . *Don't do it*. At least for now. Wait until your kid is a solid sleeper, and you're on solid footing with your spouse, before venturing off your home turf. There's no such thing as a relaxing vacation if it involves traveling with a baby. And if you happen to dislike your in-laws already, just wait until they make you schlep your kid across country for a holiday visit. It'll make it so your vows, "'til death do you part" won't come soon enough.

When you travel, you have everything working against you. The travel day itself is stressful because you have to lug a U-Haul's worth of crap with you. If you're lucky enough to have your kid nap the whole way in the car or airplane, your good fortune will come back to bite you on your sleepless bee-hind when you're up with your kid that night. If you go through a time zone, you'll have to deal with a kid who's up at the crack of dawn or goes to sleep later than you do. If you're in a hotel, you either have to figure out that complex port-a-crib or deal with the hotel crib, which will look like something out of a Joan Crawford movie, and smell even worse. (Note: This might be a good time to try the old sock-drawer trick.)

> **❝**I flew with my two-year-old last month, and the only way to get him to stop crying was if I let him have some gum, something I'd never normally do. By the time we landed, he had eaten a pack and a half's worth, and I learned that swallowed gum doesn't stay in your system for seven years like the old wives believe, and I have the diaper to prove it.**❞**
>
> —Leslie

Worst of all, if you stay with your in-laws, they'll have set up the hand-me-down crib complete with chipping lead-based paint and slats that are wide enough to trap your baby's head. You'll want to decline, but your husband will give you one of those "Don't your dare say anything that will upset my mother" looks, and you'll shoot him the "Die right now, you stupid idiot" look in return.

If you don't have a choice because you're forced to travel for work, emergency, or because of a really good parental guilt trip, then here are a few helpful tips:

Top 10 Tips for Parents Who Travel with Babies

1. If your baby sleeps better in bed with you, bring her in and kick your husband out. My husband has slept in many a hotel room bathtub and closet.

2. If you travel to a place in a different time zone, try to keep your baby on his home schedule if you're not going to be gone very long. It will make your return home much more pleasant.

3. Abandon any and all plans to get your kid to sleep though the night. The only thing you'll get with the "cry it out" method is an ugly scene with a total stranger in a hotel hallway at three in the morning.

4. On vacation, do not attempt any ridiculous projects such as weaning or potty training. Getting your kid to sleep will be more than enough to deal with.

5. All previous rules go out the window. Just do anything that works—nipples, bottles, boobs, dancing girls—*anything*.

6. Stick to your baby's bedtime routine. After all, the beauty of the five Bs is that they're completely portable.

7. Bring as much from home as you can. Familiarity breeds contentment—that CD

of lullabies, a favorite stuffed animal, Fee Fee the family poodle—whatever you can stuff into the suitcase.

8. Get a bigger suitcase.

9. If your baby is ill, don't forget to bring medications. The only thing worse than a crying baby in the middle of the night is trying to find an all-night pharmacy in a strange town with a crying baby in the middle of the night.

10. If your baby has a cold, have your pediatrician check out his ears before getting on a plane. If you're lucky, there may be an ear infection brewing, which is your "get out of jail free" card. Flying with an ear infection is a great big no-no since it can cause the eardrum to burst. Even if there isn't, just say that there is. What? Like your in-laws'll really be able to tell.

11. *Bonus tip*: Have a friend call you and fake an emergency so you have to return home *now*!

Once you get back to your home sweet home, be prepared for your baby to continue to resist sleeping. After all, his schedule has gone haywire, and we won't even go into the jet lag or any nasty germs that he contracted on the plane. It's all just too ugly.

Bottom line? Beg and plead for people to come to *you*—at least until your kid is old enough to book his own flight. And while this might create some conflict now, it will be worth it in the long run for the sake of family relations. After all, *you're* the parents now, and you can decide how vacations are dictated.

Close to You

Until your kid was about six months old, she thought that you and she were one and the same. The two of you were the yin and yang, Oprah and Gayle, Dolce and Gabbana. But somewhere between six and twelve months, it will dawn on your child that the two of you are actually two separate people. And that realization will scare the mustard-colored crap out of her.

The degree of separation anxiety varies in children. Some don't mind being handed off to a new sitter, while others freak out when you step into the bathroom. And if you have a kid like the latter, you can expect her to have a harder time spending the night all by her little lonesome. You can't really blame her really—I mean, hey, how many of us broke up with boyfriends past their expiration dates just to avoid the same scenario—but it's still not a desire you want to indulge.

When separation anxiety begins, your baby will try every conceivable way she can to climb back inside your uterus. She'll want to be held more than usual and be by your side wherever you go. And at night, she'll cry for you to be with her. While it will be sweet at first to feel so needed, soon it will get as old as your husband's empty promises to help out more around the house. Especially when your baby cries for you every two hours, night after night after night.

I understand that in your wild and maternal imagination, your innocent child feels as abandoned, rejected, and unloved as you were when you were skipped over for the prom and had to go with your geeky cousin, but, get over it, sister! Separation anxiety is very normal, and like all other developmental stages, it too will pass (to make way for yet another frustrating aspect of parenting). Until it does, give your child some extra snuggles and reassurance during the daylight hours and extra cuddles and one-on-one attention before bedtime. If she calls out for you, try different things. Maybe just a shout-out of "Mommy's here" will do the trick. Or you may have to go in and reassure her that you're still around, but only stay for a moment. Eventually she'll get the picture that you're not going any-where, and she will stop being so clingy. Yes, one day in the not-too-distant future, she'll even be begging you to "puleez!" just leave her alone. And when that day comes, it's then that you'll wish you could return to these exhausting, yet good old days of separation anxiety.

Who'll Let the Dog Out? Who? Who? Who? Who? Who?

As soon as you bring your baby home from the hospital, man's best friend turns into Mommy's worst nightmare. That's because after hours of rocking and walking, and nursing and cursing, you *finally* get your baby to sleep, just as Fido barks ferociously at the evil burglar disguised as your mail carrier. Now the dog is barking, and the baby is screaming, and you're having a tin-gling sensation in your left arm. You decide that your stamina isn't strong enough for both baby and dog, and one of them has to go! Since there will come a day when you don't have to clean up your kid's poop, but you'll eternally have to clean up your dog's, you go with the dog.

But before you kick Fido to the curb, take a deep breath and try to see things from his point of view. Poor Fido. He has no idea why you're screaming at him. He's only doing his job, and he's been doing it for the past three years to your glowing affection and praise. Before you had a baby, your dog *was* your baby. You gave him baths, cuddled in bed, and even spoke to him in baby talk, the reasons non–dog owners will never understand. But now that you've brought home that demanding and funny-smelling thing, everything has changed. Your new baby gets all of your attention, and your dog feels as neglected as your husband did during your pregnancy.

When dealing with a dog and a new baby, it's best to have the dog get used to the baby even before it arrives. Teach it commands like "hush" whenever he barks (see "Resources" on page 196), not to jump up on people coming to your home, and have him get familiar with new baby smells and sounds (like baby lotion and the sound of a rattle). Take your dog to the vet before the baby's born to check him for parasites or any other health concerns that might prevent him from being close to the baby. Then, the night when your kid is born, have Dad bring home the blanket that the baby was wrapped up in, and have your dog smell it. Dog's noses are so keen, he can probably detect your kid's middle name!

" When our second child was born, I brought his first dirty diaper home from the hospital for our dog to smell. I thought this would get him used to the baby's smell, but all it did was teach me that we better get a good diaper pail because our dog took off with the diaper and shredded it to pieces. **"**

—Julia

If you've already brought your baby home, there are still some things that you can do to assure that both pet and Petunia will all get along. If you have an especially fussy baby, or an especially vocal animal, this might take more finesse than you feel capable of doing right now, but I'm afraid you have no choice. Okay, I guess you do have a choice, but let's see what we can do to make things better before we go down that ugly road of giving away your beloved family pet:

- Put your dog outside when it's naptime. Just make sure that there's some shade on hot days, shelter on rainy days, and a bowl of water on all days. If he still barks too loudly outside, put him in an empty room inside the house. Yes, you'll feel guilty, but if you toss in a treat with him each time, your dog may actually look forward to this alone time.

- Use a white noise machine in the baby's room when she goes down for a nap. This will provide some continuous sound so that your dog's sudden barking won't be so disturbing. Nor, for that matter, will your soap opera with the loud quarrel by the evil twin who put her good twin in a coma after the DNA proved that her baby wasn't hers, but in fact was her sister's who got pregnant while having amnesia.

- If your dog freaks out whenever someone comes to the door, put a sign on your driveway or mailbox that reads, "No Solicitors," or "No Visitors Please," or even "Don't You Dare Ring the Doorbell or Else I'll Kill You with My Own Bare Hands!"

- Muzzle—I really don't like the idea of using muzzles, especially for an extended period of time. But if you're desperate, and you use them only during naptime, and get one that's well fitted and allows your dog to drink and pant, then, I guess I can look the other way.

No matter what you do to quiet the scene, make sure to give Fido extra love and attention during the adjustment phase. Also, be sure to praise him often when he's acting well behaved around the baby. Not only will this make him happy, but it will nip any jealousy issues that will be much harder to deal with than some errant barking. When things get tough, think of the big picture: your child and your beloved dog growing up together, playing fetch, and becoming best buds for years to come. And yes, with you not far behind picking up Fido's poop.

Change in Routine

Let's face it, babies are not the most easy-going creatures in the world. And where sleep is concerned, "structure" is the name of the game. Nevertheless, life happens, and a tiny ripple in our day-to-day can feel like a tsunami to babies who thrive on predictability. Yes, many things are out of your control, but some things aren't, and you should bear this in mind when planning your day. Should any of the following occur, they may be huge disruptions to the routine that you've worked so hard to create. And you can expect to hear about it from your baby—at three in the morning. . . .

Top 10 Bedtime-Routine Busters

1. **One parent has to go out of town.** If you broke the cardinal rule and made a parent a part of your baby's sleep routine, then you're in for it. When Daddy's not around to do the woo-woo dance in order for your kid to fall asleep, there's going to be hell to pay. And considering that you're already resentful because Daddy can sleep eight continuous hours in a quiet hotel room, you don't need any more stress in your life.

2. **Houseguests.** The problem with houseguests is that they need to be entertained. Since most refuse to kick in for the rental car when they visit, it's up to you (and therefore your kid) to schlep them around the city from morning to night visiting all the tourist attractions. That translates into missed naps, late bedtimes, and noisy homes after Baby's bedtime. But then again, it still beats having to go visit them.

3. **Home construction.** What, are you nuts? You have a baby at home! Don't top it off with a home remodel.

4. **Daylight-saving time.** This alone makes me want to move to Arizona until my child is ten years old.

5. **A new babysitter or day care.** This change will be as upsetting for your kid as McDonald's new "healthier" yet not-as-good-tasting fries was for you.

6. **Another baby.** Oh, for God's sake! How can you expect Baby Number One to sleep through the night, when Baby Number Two won't stop crying? Didn't your doctor warn you that the whole "you can't get pregnant when you're breastfeeding" thing is a myth?!

7. **Mommy's return to work.** Tortuous for both you and your baby.

8. **A new pet.** Again, are you nuts?!

9. **Moving to a new home.** Now I'm just plain disgusted. Don't you know that one of the most stressful things you can do, besides divorce and death, is to move? And moving *with* a baby will most definitely cause a divorce if it doesn't kill you first.

10. **Divorce.** You didn't listen to me about the moving thing, did you?

I Gave Birth to a Farmer!

One of the darkest periods I had getting my daughter to sleep through the night was when she would continually wake up at five in the morning raring to go for the day. I say "darkest" because, well, it was dark. Pitch-dark in fact, as it always is at such an ungodly hour. Whenever I'd consult my parenting books, they'd all tell me the same thing: Five o'clock is technically sleeping through the night. Well, I'm here to tell you that they're full of pitooey. Waking up before *Sesame Street* does not constitute sleeping through the night!

The books would offer some suggestions in hopes of getting her to sleep longer, but none of them worked. The most common: Put her to sleep later at night in hopes of her waking up later in the morning. But no matter how late I'd put her down, she'd still wake up at the crack of dawn, along with duck hunters and garbage collectors, ready to start her busy day. She had places to go, things to do, and milk to drink. Waking up at five in the morning may be fine for moms who have jobs as morning news anchors or go to sunrise services, but it's not for me. And if you're anything like me, it's not for you either.

If putting your baby down later at night doesn't solve the problem, here are a few things you can try in hopes of sleeping in a bit more:

- If your baby isn't in four-alarm hysterics, wait a few minutes before you get her out of the crib. This will, you hope, give her the opportunity to entertain herself, or better yet, fall back asleep out of boredom.

- If you can't resist running in her room at the first peep, turn off the baby monitor. Don't worry. Unless you have you have your kid sleep in the guest house on the other side of your five-acre compound, you should have no trouble hearing her if she really cries.

- Get black-out shades for the baby's room. If the nursery has an east-facing room that lets in the dawn's early light, block it out.

- Resist feeding her the first thing in the morning. If your child is used to getting breakfast at 5:00 A.M. every day, her tummy is going to want food at 5:00 A.M. every day. Push breakfast a little later every morning.

- On the same note, feed her as late as possible and even top her off when it's your bedtime (depending on her age and if she even needs to eat in the middle of the night at all).

- Wait until daylight-saving time begins, so that 5:00 A.M. instantly becomes 6:00 A.M. and you get to sleep in one more hour! And hope this schedule will stick and your problem will be solved. Tired moms love the beginning of daylight-saving time. "It's the most wonderful time of the year!"

If none of these suggestions do the trick, you can try the following *desperate measures* to get a little more sleep:

- Take your baby into bed with you when she wakes up: This could buy you another thirty minutes.
- Put on the TV, put your baby in the play-pen, turn on PBS, and lie down on the sofa for a few minutes of shuteye. There will always be something on that will engage your baby, even if it's their yearly telethon. I'm convinced the people who work for this station have babies at home and know how desperately we need them at five in the morning. Bless you, PBS.
- Cheerios: If your baby is old enough for solids, he can be occupied for a good chunk of time with these brilliant little circles. But do not leave him unattended.
- Triple Fudge Desperation Supreme: A combination of these three that, I swear, will help get your through the first two years of your kid's life. Take your baby into bed with you, put on the TV, and give her a

cup of Cheerios. Then you zone out in that stage that's 50 percent asleep, and 50 percent awake and aware of what your baby's doing in case she wanders too close to the edge of the bed. I'm not saying it's neat. I'm not saying it's pretty. I'm not saying it's honorable. But it does work, and really—isn't that all that matters right now?

- Tell your husband to deal with it. He has to be up for work soon anyway (assuming you're a stay-at-home mom. If not, then tell your husband to deal with it anyway).

chapter 8

toddler troubles

Now that your baby has become a toddler, he's doing it all. He's walking (all over you) and running (you ragged). He's even talking, although at this early stage, you're the only one who can understand him. I call this "Lassie" talk because it reminds me of the old TV show when Lassie would bark, and only Timmy would be able to understand what he said.

"Woof, woof," barked Lassie.

"Oh no!" exclaimed Timmy. "Johnny fell in the well and you need a strong rope and a team of horses to get him out?"

Hand in hand with your kid's latest miracles come your kid's latest sleeping problems. Along with a baby who can walk comes a baby who can climb out of his crib. Along with a baby who can feed himself comes a baby who wants to feed himself at three in the morning. And along with a baby who can talk comes a little monster who can insist that he's not tired and will not be going to bed tonight or any other night, thank you very much!

"Will all this madness ever end?" you cry in a fit of impatient, exhausted despair. "Will I ever be able to sleep for eight continuous hours on a consistent basis as I did before I made my now-questionable decision to procreate?" The answer, my friend, is perhaps. But it will have more to do with your behavior than that of your child. If you're strong and can stand up to an adorable toddler who has the face of an angel and the voice of someone who just sucked a helium balloon, than perhaps you will. But if you want to savor every moment of toddlerhood because you know in the not-too-distant future, the only bedtime calls you'll be getting are the long-distance kind from college asking you for more money, then you can expect problems.

So here's to toddlerhood, with all of its miracles, and yes, all of its accompanying sleeping problems.

Nightmares

Nightmares are one of the most insidious con-
tributors to toddler sleep issues, and as far as I'm
concerned, one big booboo in the grand design of
the universe. They serve no purpose at all except
to scare children, torment their sleepy parents,
and make zillions of dollars for the creator of the
Chucky movies.

At around three years of age, almost all children will have experienced nightmares at one
time or another. Some children may have them for
days on end, while others have them very infre-
quently. But no matter how often they occur, all
children wake up in despair. As adults, we're able
to distinguish between real and fake (except for
men and silicone boobs, or maybe they just don't
care). We can calm ourselves by saying "it was
only a dream." Little ones don't grasp this concept and therefore freak out. To the growing toddler brain, frightened and alone in a dark room in
the middle of the night, dreams and reality can
become one and the same.

Toddler brains can be sent to that scary zone
by a number of things: big changes in routine,
potty training, too much action before bedtime,
divorce, or moving to a new home. Or, they can

be brought on by a tomato. A big, red tomato that Roo threw at Pooh in the latest Disney film. And oh, how terrifying that tomato can be to a toddler with an irrational fear. Every child I've ever encountered has one whether it is toward an evil form of produce or a child-eating drain hole. And even though these fears may sound silly to us grown people, they are quite a serious matter to our little ones.

Another culprit in the breeding of nightmares is Junior's ever-growing imagination. A toddler's brain develops much faster than his sense of reason, and Junior's active imagination doesn't go to sleep when he does. Therefore his dreams are an entertaining way of shining a light on the problems he's dealing with during the day. Yes, there are plenty of therapists who'll give you Freudian, Jungian, or bullsh*tian theory as to what a particular dream means, but who cares if the goblin's nose represents you or his brand-new potty chair. Nightmares suck, regardless of what characters play in the theater of your child's mind.

If your kid is especially fearful, talk to him about his anxiety. If he's terrified of daddy long-legs, explain that a daddy longlegs doesn't have teeth and can't hurt him. Also, see if you can catch one and put it in a glass container so that he can look at it close up. Education can go a long way to

❝ I have such a fearful child. Yes, she's scared of big things like amusement park rides and bees. But she's also freaked out by the slanted letter *M* that's on the end logo of *Zoboomafoo*. If she catches even a second of that show, she screams in fear and races out of the room. **❞**

—Joan

ease fears. If your child's fear is that of the all-too-common "monster," here are some ideas to keep it at bay (if they only worked on telemarketers):

1. **Monster checks.** You and your child do a full sweep of the room to make sure "all's clear."

2. **Incantations.** You and your child can recite your own magic spell to keep the boogies at bay.

3. **Monster spray.** Put water in a spray bottle and spray it around the room. If desired, add a relaxing scent like lavender. (Note: If your child's room smells a bit ripe from dirty socks or stinky dogs, use Febreze as your spray bottle. It'll wipe out monsters, and that musty smell.)

4. **Security guards.** Assign a stuffed animal the task of guarding the room. If your kids believe in monsters, they may also believe that teddy bears are bestowed with magical powers that scare off ghosts.

5. **Little siblings.** The presence of another living thing in the room can alleviate even the most unreasonable fears. And besides, siblings have to be good for something.

When a child cries in fear from having a nightmare, go to him quickly. This is not the time to let him cry it out and let his running imagination do even more damage. Console him. Listen to him if he wants to talk about his dream. Reassure him that he's safe and that dreams are just make-believe. Resist the temptation to take him into bed with you since there are sure to be many more nightmares in his future. Instead, stay with him until he's calmed down, or maybe until he's asleep if his nightmare was really disturbing.

Obviously the best way to deal with a nightmare is to prevent it altogether, and if I could do that, I'd be like that millionaire mommy who invented the stroller cup holder. But alas, the answer eludes me. Still, there are a few common-sense precautions you can take to keep the nightmares at bay:

- Have a calm pre-bedtime routine. No raucous games of "bloody monster," or "there's a kid-eating dragon under your bed."
- Equally, no scary books. Harry Potter and toddlers do not mix.
- If you must watch TV, make sure that it's a cuddly and soft program that has no scary tomatoes.

Keep in mind that nightmares, like all other aspects of a child's life, are ripe for manipulation. Once your kid learns that having a nightmare warrants having you race into his room with lots of attention and TLC, be prepared for your method actor to put on a performance every night. And that'll be a nightmare of a different kind!

Night Terrors

Night terrors are like nightmares on Miracle-Gro. They're scarier and more stressful to endure than any simple nightmare. For you anyway. For your kid, they're a non-event since most children don't remember having a night terror come morning time. You, on the other hand, will never forget it.

There are only two things that night terrors have with in common with nightmares. One is that they'll have you waking up to the sound of your child screaming. The other is that when you get to your child, he'll be inconsolable. But much more so than with just any ordinary nightmare. He'll be highly agitated, possibly even sweating, breathing fast, shaking, and panic stricken. And, unlike with an ordinary nightmare, he'll also be fast asleep.

Dealing with it can be quite disturbing. You can look right at your child, but he won't know that you're there. You can talk to him, but he won't be able to hear you. In fact, your child will be in such a deep state of sleep, that he won't act the same. And, because he's in such a deep sleep during a night terror, it's not a good idea to wake him up because the transition could be too upsetting. Just stay with your child until the night terror passes and he's back to his normal sleep pattern. While you're with him, prevent him from falling out of bed, hurting himself in any way, or running to a field and howling at the moon.

It's estimated that about 15 percent of all children between the ages of two and six will get night terrors. Night terrors usually last between ten and thirty minutes, but if they last much longer, you should call your pediatrician. No one knows exactly what causes them. Some experts believe that they're brought on by temporary problems in the nervous system when your child sleeps. Others say that they're triggered when the child is overtired. That should be reason enough not to veer too far off of your kid's sleeping schedule.

Like most childhood conditions—such as sleepwalking or an obsession to read the same book over and over again until you want to put a bullet through your head—this too will pass. But until it does, deal with them the best you can and make sure to warn any overnight sitters so that they won't panic and run outside to look for the mother ship.

From Crib to Bed to Who Knows Where

One question that every parent of a toddler asks himself is if it's legal to leave your kid alone in the house and run to the liquor store when he's having a full-blown tantrum? Another question is when is the right time to get the child a big-kid bed. And although the answer to the first question is no (even if you really, really want to), the answer to the second question isn't nearly so cut and dried.

Yes, you'll need to get a big-kid bed if your child is old enough to climb out of the crib by himself. You'll also need to get one if there's a new baby due soon and you don't want to cough up the cash for crib number two. But if neither of those scenarios is true, I suggest that you keep your kid in his crib until his feet grow long enough to stick through the slats. That's because a contained baby is a safe baby, and one who doesn't have the sleeping problems that big-kid bed owners do. Once a kid hits that mattress unrestrained, all bets are off. When it comes to choosing a bed for your toddler, there are several options.

1. **A toddler bed.** This is a bed that's not much larger than the crib mattress. In fact, if you thought ahead when you bought your crib, you chose one that had the capability of transforming into an actual toddler bed when the time arose. Of course most new parents can't fathom the idea that their itty-bitty newborns will actually grow into toddlers one day.

2. **A twin bed.** I've found that the majority of parents go for this option. Even if they use the toddler bed as a transition, they choose a twin bed next for their next purchase. A twin bed is smaller than a double and leaves more space for play in the room.

Also, a twin bed is only big enough to fit one person, so it limits overnight guests!

3. **A double bed.** This was our bed of choice. Yes, it did cost more and took up more space in the room, but it does have advantages. A double bed is comfortable for both parent and child to fit in for bedtime readings and sick nights. And as your child gets older, a double bed is great for sleepovers.

4. **The actual crib mattress.** If you have a hard time deciding between paper and plastic, you may need more time to make your decision. In the meantime, just take out the crib mattress and stick it on the floor. Sure, it makes it easy for your kid to crawl out of at night, but there's no worry that he'll fall out of bed and break a bone either!

No matter what kind of big-kid bed you choose, the problems will all be the same. To begin with, putting a big-kid bed in your child's room is like setting up a carnival fun ride. He'll want to climb on board and jump up and down till he pukes. Sure he used to jump in his crib, but now that he's got acres of jumping space, he'll go hog-wild! That's why it's important to plug up any nooks and crannies between the bed and the wall that could trap a foot and cause

injury. If you have a head and foot board, make
sure that there are no sharp edges that he can fall
on and hurt himself. If so, you'll need to do some
babyproofing.

Another problem with a big-kid bed is that
once you tuck your toddler in it, he can come and
go as he pleases. And in the middle of the night,
what pleases him most is to be with you. Yes,
you can get guardrails and you should, but they
only prevent your child from falling out . . . not
getting out. That's why part of your new bedtime
ritual will be to clean up all the toys and treasures
that are on the floor between his room and yours
that he could step on. You should also light up
the path like an airport runway so that he can see
where he's going. Also, it wouldn't hurt to start
locking your door whenever you and your hubby
have sex to avoid those awkward conversations
trying to convince your kid that Daddy didn't
actually hurt Mommy.

But by far the biggest problem you'll face
with a big-kid bed isn't one of safety, but one of
sanity. Now that your child realizes that he has
the magical power of getting out of bed at will,
he'll use this power as much as he can get away
with. (Note: There are a few kids, however, who
don't realize they have this power. They stay
locked in their beds as if they were islands in

shark-infested seas and yell for their parents to come to their rooms instead. No, this is not a reflection of their IQs.)

After a few weeks, the novelty of having a big-kid bed will wear off, just like all those Christmas toys that he wanted soooooo badly and then stopped playing with five minutes after they came out of the boxes. It's at this point that you can crawl in bed with your man and feel proud that you've crossed yet another milestone in the healthy development of your child. Give your-selves a good pat on the back. You've earned it. Perhaps even a hug. (Be careful with this one. Your husband is so starved for affection that even an accidental touch while crossing paths will send him into a frenzy of sexual desire.) Then roll over and wait for the next speed bump of sleep-ing problems to hit, because now that your child has been let loose upon the world, *anything* can happen.

I Can't Sleep, If Sleeping Is Without You

Okay, so maybe you don't have a problem with your child getting out of bed. Once she's in, she stays like a well-trained show dog. The problem, however, is that she wants *you* to stay there with her so she won't be alone. Having a kid who wants you to lie in bed with her until she falls asleep is a common and frustrating problem and can turn bedtime into helltime.

This is your normal nighttime ritual: You read your child a book, give her a kiss good night, and tell her that you'll see her in the morning. But as you get up to leave, she starts the whining, the begging, and the chokehold to get you to stay. Not wanting to upset her right before bedtime, you concede and lie next to her in total silence. As you will her to fall asleep, you think of the sink full of dirty dishes, the laundry that still needs folding, and the alone time that you could be spending with your husband when you don't have to spell out certain words. Finally, she makes those pre-sleep twitching movements, which is your cue to am-scray. Ever so carefully you tiptoe out of her room, but you step on a damn squeaky floorboard, and now she's wide-awake. Busted!

There are several reasons you've suddenly become your child's newest and bestest security object. One is that she's having problems falling asleep by herself. If so, a nice back rub helps, as does asking her to close her eyes while you tell her relaxing things to envision. If she's too wound up, instill a fifteen-minute "calm down" period before bedtime each night when she can not partake in any rowdy activity.

Another reason for your child's clinginess is that she may be dealing with fears. If it's monsters she's afraid of, use monster spray or any other suggestion on page 163. If she's afraid of the dark, keep the lights on. Yes, all of them. Install stadium lights if you have to, if it helps getting your kid to sleep.

Once you've figured out the problem and dealt with it, try using baby steps. Stay with her until she's almost asleep. Then, get up to leave, and tell her that you'll be back in three minutes to check on her. Oftentimes, just knowing that you're coming back will give your child enough peace of mind to let you go. After you return to check on her, tell her you'll be back in five minutes. Gradually keep adding on until you only have to check on her every twelve minutes (the time between commercial breaks).

If she insists on having you stay, don't become a playmate. In fact, set some ground rules. Tell your child that she cannot talk while you're there. She cannot play. And she cannot open her eyes. Chances are, she'll be asleep in no time once she stays still. Either that, or she'll be so bored having you around, that she'll push you out the door.

Sleepwalking

Sleepwalking has gotten a bad rap thanks to old-fashioned sitcoms like *Gilligan's Island* and *I Dream of Jeannie* that loved using this device to create comedic high jinks. Forget the images of George Jefferson wandering around with outstretched arms in his dee-lux apartment in the sky. That's not how it works at all. It's more of a simple, aimless ambling without any Frankenstein qualities whatsoever, and no laugh track accompaniment (except for a few giggles from you because it's so dang funny).

Sleepwalking is actually a normal and common occurrence in children. It usually begins in toddlerhood when a child can finally walk freely about the house. It can last anywhere from a couple of months to a few years, and it is more of an inconvenience than a condition that merits worry. But don't fret, sleepwalking generally passes on its own without much fanfare.

There are no warning signs of sleepwalking. One night you'll bolt awake thinking some stranger is at the foot of your bed only to find your kid having a full-on conversation in some strange, gibberish language. Don't panic. Don't force your child to wake up. And don't call in an exorcist to rid him of his satanic tongue. Simply guide him back to his room, speak a few soft, reassuring words, and tuck him back into bed. Chances are he'll mumble a few humorous non-sequiturs, drift off to sleep, and not remember any of it in the morning. You won't remember much of it either because you'll have to take a couple strong sleeping pills in order to fall back to sleep after the panic of thinking someone was in your house.

If you have a nocturnal wanderer in your midst, the main thing to be concerned about is childproofing. You must be hypervigilant about any potential hazards your nighttime nomad could encounter. Also, if there are any forbidden items around the house that he's learned not to touch during the day, it's best to put them

❝I consider my husband, Rudy, to be a very smart man. But he thought of this asinine idea of tying one end of a string to our son's toe and the other to his. He thought by doing this, he'd know when our son was sleepwalking. The only thing that happened is we awoke to our son tangled up in string and fast asleep in bed next to us.❞

—Margaret

on high shelves. Kids come up with the dang-
est excuses for breaking things, but being asleep
while they're doing it is a pretty darn good one.

Whatever you do, don't be tempted to restrain
your toddler in his bed, or contain him in his room
in any sort of scary way. Not only is it just plain
cruel, but it could cause your child to have nightmares, which would make you lose even more
sleep. After a few sleepwalking incidences, you
won't panic to find your kid wandering around
the house in the wee hours of night. In fact, you
may even look forward to it. After you get him
back to bed, you can turn on the tube and watch
some of those classic TV shows that are on at that
hour. They really are quite hysterical!

Two's Company, Three's a Crowd . . . in Bed

There's something about a parent's bed that's as
addictive as iced blended mochas. Once your kid
gets a taste of how warm and snug and loving
it is to sleep with his folks, that habit will be as
difficult to break as . . . well, as those delicious
iced blended mochas. When your little cuddle
monster comes to you in the wee hours of the
morn, all sleepy and sweet, with hair like a dan-
delion and breath like cotton candy, it's so easy to

grab him, pull him into bed with you, snuggle, cuddle, and deal with it in the morning! But, if a good night's sleep is what you want, this habit should be nipped in the bud.

Yes, there's nothing as picturesque as a toddler sleeping in between the people who helped make him. There's also nothing as uncomfortable. After just a few minutes of having this threesome, your arm gets numb, your leg cramps up, and you're forced to lie like a pencil at the edge of the bed, inches from falling off. You don't dare move for fear of waking up your toddler and having to deal with having to put him back to sleep again, so you stay awake all night in this locked position.

That's why, as much as your kid will protest, you shouldn't allow him to get in the habit of sleeping in your room. Sure, I could say something about how getting your child to sleep in his own room will foster independence and self-confidence. Maybe it will. But independence shmindependence. The main reason to get your kid out of your bed is that there isn't room enough in your bed for three, despite your husband's fantasies to the contrary. Besides, there may even be times when you and your mate want to, well . . . mate, and having a kid in between you is more of an obstacle than doing it when you're having your period. And finally, since you went to all the time, trouble, and expense of decorating the baby's room as an exact replica of baby Shiloh Jolie-Pitt's, you need a kid in there to complete the picture.

There are many reasons that your child wants to come into your room in the middle of the night. Like any other sleeping problem, it's best to find out the cause so that you can find a cure. Here are some of the common causes of nocturnal visits:

- A big change in your child's routine such as travel, moving to a new home, or a new brand of apple juice.
- Milestones such as teething, potty training, or starting preschool.
- Any sort of anxiety or fear a toddler might develop, which could range from asparagus to zebras.
- Nightmares.
- He hasn't learned to fall asleep by himself when he wakes up at night.
- Illness.
- Because it's Thursday. Sometimes they just go to their parents' rooms for absolutely no rhyme or reason whatsoever.

Yes, I know you're exhausted. You've worked a ten-hour day, went grocery shopping, cleaned the house, and ran to the groomers to get the dog's anal gland expressed. I know your back is killing you, and all you need is a little shuteye so that everything will be all right in the morning. But still, you must get up and walk that kid back to bed. Over and over and over if necessary—otherwise, if you allow it to happen just one time, he'll keep coming back again and again . . . just as I do with those delicious iced mochas. Be consistent, be patient, and most of all, be strong. Don't make a fuss (you don't want Junior to wake up too much). Don't get angry (you don't want Junior to feel rejected). Just calmly walk Junior back into his room and tuck him back in bed.

If it's too late and your kid is already accustomed to sleeping in your bed, might I suggest a compromise? Set up a separate sleeping area in your room where your child can nest. Unroll a sleeping bag or lay down some blankets and a pillow, and let your child climb in by himself whenever he needs to. Sure, he'll be in your room, but you'll be asleep the whole time so what the hell do you care? Genius I tell ya, pure genius!

A Little Whine Before Bed

It's finally here. The moment you've been waiting for since breakfast. It's your kid's bedtime! You've been counting down the minutes as if it were the last day of school before summer vacation, and the bell finally rang! You track down your kid and tell her that it's bedtime, but instead of complying, she informs you in no uncertain terms that it ain't gonna happen. No way. No how.

Here you are, so worn out from the day that you can barely communicate with any life form higher than your child's pet goldfish, and it's at this exact moment that your toddler fights you the most. Man, she's gooood! But before you take matters in your own hands and do something that's frowned upon by Social Services, take a moment to breathe and understand what's going on in that immature brain of hers. She's not being difficult for difficult sake. She's just too busy to go to sleep. The world is an E-ticket ride and there are so many places to explore, bookcases to climb, walls to paint, and watches to flush. Really now, could you fall asleep in the middle of a once-a-year clearance sale at Anthropologie? I think not.

Sure, you can try reasoning with your stubborn kid. But that's as futile at trying to talk the sour out of a grapefruit. But if you put it in toddlerspeak, *and* if your child is motivated, you may actually get somewhere. For instance, if your kid is into superheroes, tell her they need to sleep in order for their muscles to grow big and strong. This will no doubt come back to bite you when your kid neurotically measures her biceps every morning, but you'll deal with it another day. Right now, it's time for bed!

Once you convince your child to go to bed, it's important to prepare for the inevitable. Intercept all the obvious last-ditch requests that your child will ask for once you walk out the bedroom door. Make sure that she's used the bathroom (if she's potty trained), brushed her teeth, has some water on her nightstand in case she gets thirsty, and has her security object in hand. If there are any monster worries, check the closets, look under the bed for gremlins, and use the monster spray when needed. Yes, getting ready for bedtime will be as detailed a mission as a security sweep by the Secret Service, but an ounce of prevention is worth a pound of excuses as to why your child can't fall asleep.

Even with these preventive measures, you'll be amazed at how many times your little one comes out of bed in the hope of manipulating you into letting her stay up. She'll look at you with the face of a princess and the voice of Cindy Lou Who. She'll sit on your lap, stroke your face, and tell you that you're the greatest mommy in the whole entire universe. She'll give a performance that will rival Vivien Leigh in *Gone with the Wind*. That's why, when your little drama queen comes out for a curtain call, be firm. Don't get mad, but don't be a sucker either. Repeat after me, "It's bedtime now. We'll talk about it tomorrow." Be proud that your toddler is so brilliant and clever. Then give her a kiss and walk her back to her room.

Oh, it won't be easy. You're dealing with a worthy opponent who knows exactly how to get what she wants. She's been studying you and knows just how to push your "awww, how cute" buttons. Just know that if you let her get away with it even one time, she'll come back with more stamina than Rob Lowe in his infamous sex video.

You should also know that these "butidon't-wannas" aren't just reserved for nighttime. They rear their ugly heads during naptime as well. Sometimes it can take longer to get your kid to nap than the nap itself. But sleep she must, for a well-rested child makes for a happy child, a happy child makes for an easier bedtime, and on and on it goes. Again, Mother Nature has designed it to work this way, and you can't fight Mother Nature. If you don't believe me, just look at your husband's expanding waistline!

Urine for Trouble

So you've finally gotten your toddler to sleep through the night—congratulations. And you've finally gotten him potty trained—fabulous. But don't think that these two milestones necessarily go hand in hand. There may be plenty of times that you'll get a wake-up call in the middle of the night to change a set of soggy sheets, for as you know, it's hard to sleep on a wet spot.

The "average" age that a child is able to sleep through the night and wake up dry is three years old. Some babies do it as early as two, and a few can even achieve this miraculous goal at one (although the parents should keep this information to themselves if they want to keep their friends). On the other extreme, some kids have accidents until they're six years old, some even later. It's really all a crapshoot, or should I say, "pee shoot," as night dryness is purely the byproduct of things such as a mature bladder. And, as we learned in grade school when boys would turn their eyelids inside out just to get our attention, boys tend to mature later than girls. Also, some toddlers tend to sleep deeper than others and may not be able to recognize the signal that they have to "go." Regardless of why it happens, bed-wetting is a normal developmental stage that'll keep you up at night, fill your hampers with wet bedding, and worst of all, force you to fold a lot of fitted sheets!

Unfortunately, when it comes to bed-wetting, there's not a lot you can do to prevent it. Sure, you can avoid having your kid drink a super-size jug of liquid before it's time for lights out. Or you can invest in a bed-wetting alarm that will go off as soon as it gets wet, waking up your child in a panic. Yes, your kid may have fewer accidents, but that may be because your kid is so traumatized by the alarm that he's petrified to fall asleep.

On that note, you should also know that no amount of bullying, intimidation, bribes, or prizes are going to make a child stay dry at night either. It's not as if your child is choosing to pee all over himself. He's asleep. Yelling at him or offering him candy if he stops will only add to the pressure. And between the stress of learning how to share and not being able to bite his brother whenever he wants, he has enough pressures to deal with as it is.

So stop talking about it. Don't make a big deal about it. And put the night diapers back on. Do your kid and your utility bill a great big favor, and don't take them off again until your kid is good and ready. By "good and ready," I mean after he's had several nights of waking up in dry diapers, he tells you that he wants to sleep in underpants, he wakes up dry consistently after naps, and his mattress has had a chance to dry out.

Having said that, when you do enter the land of diaper-free nights, invest in a good waterproof mattress pad. And, if you just can't force yourself to change yet another set of soggy sheets in the middle of the night, just throw a couple of towels over the puddle and deal with it in the morning. Yes, I know it sounds gross, but it's a lot more hygienic than having your kid sleep on the dog's bed. And believe me, at 3:00 A.M., even that won't sound like such a bad option.

Growing Is a Pain

Another sleeping problem that occurs in toddlers (and later on in adolescence) is growing pains. A growing pain is when your child gets a dull pain deep within the bone of either leg, anywhere from the lower calf to the upper thigh. The funny thing about growing pains is that they may have nothing to do with growing at all. My guess is that they were given this name because parents were *growing* tired of having to deal with these stupid *pains* in the wee hours of the night.

Growing pains aren't fun for anyone. You rush to your kid and find him clutching his leg and telling you that it hurts . . . a lot. When your child experiences his first growing pain, you'll search his leg for bug bites, scrapes, or abrasions, but find nothing there. Then, convinced it must be some rare, inoperable muscle tumor, you'll place a panicked call to your pediatrician like the one you made last week when you found "blood" in your kid's stool only later to remember that he ate a red crayon. I wish I could give you a quick cure for these growing pains. Believe me, I've done everything. I've tried heating pads, Bengay, massage, cold washcloths, warm washcloths, and Tylenol. But no matter what I'd try, the pain lasted for the same duration and with the same intensity.

If your child is having any other symptom besides pain—such as swelling, fever, or redness, or if the pain is located in the same spot every time—then by all means, place that panicked call to your pediatrician. Otherwise, just grin and bear it along with your child until it's over.

The Trouble with Preschool

Life is just about as perfect as it can get. Your little one is sleeping through the night and taking a long afternoon nap. Your brain has regenerated enough to perform basic tasks like calculating change and figuring out which way to set the clock when it's daylight-saving time. Yes, life is good!

Then, out of the blue, it arrives: (sound effects, please) *Crash! Schreeeech! Booom!* What the . . . ?! The *letter*. The letter from that prestigious preschool you enrolled Junior in last year that you never dreamed he'd get in. Well, surprise! He got in! Yes, after all the interviews, tours, and financial bribes, your kid is finally going to start preschool!

But then you see it. The paragraph at the bottom. The one that turns your smile upside down and informs you that your kid is enrolled in the *afternoon* session! But that's the time when he takes his three-hour nap? Why should you pay the equivalent of college tuition so that your kid can make a macaroni necklace during his naptime? This would effectively destroy the sleeping schedule that has taken you years to create.

Don't they understand that you were finally in a groove? That after years of exhaustion, you were finally starting to return people's phone calls? That just last week you actually gave someone a birthday present *on* her birthday? And that you were finally exercising again (well, okay, you were thinking about it anyway)? For God's sake, don't these people know that if your kid doesn't get his regular nap, he transforms into the Incredible Hulk? Never mind the fact that the change in routine, the new teacher, and new friends are going to completely screw up his nighttime sleep as well?

Personally, I'll never understand why a number of preschools enroll toddlers in the afternoon programs knowing full well that's the time when they take their afternoon naps. Sure, they'll tell you that your kid will adjust, but can you? Besides, you can't help but think how perfect your day would be if your kid went to preschool in the morning, came home for lunch, and then went down for a three-hour nap! Now that's a schedule you can work with!

After a day or two, you calm down and realize that, although it'll be stressful, you will get through it. Life will go on, Earth will keep spinning, and Howard Stern will continue to make controversial jokes. It'll all be worth it in the long run, and after all, the school *is* prestigious. But how do you begin to make the transition? Here are some ideas:

- A couple weeks before school is to begin, wake your kid up a little earlier each morning so that he'll go down for a nap earlier too. By the end of two weeks, he will, you hope, be able to take his nap before school even begins.

- Drive him around in the car about an hour before preschool starts so he can conk out. At least he'll get a small nap, which may tide him over until bedtime.

- Do nothing. When school starts, you'll have two weeks of hell dealing with a cranky, overtired, and overstimulated kid. After that, things will get much better. That is, until you get your first bill from the preschool!

So when your preschool says it's time to start the afternoon session, go ahead and jump for joy. Be confident that it will all be good eventually and call on your God-given gift of adaptability— the secret to the universe—or at least, to sane and happy parenting. Besides, you'll have that beautiful, handmade macaroni necklace to comfort you, so all the hell will definitely be worth it!

conclusion

good night!

One day, as you're eating your kid's leftover mac 'n cheese because it's too good to toss, you realize that you feel strangely energized. You're standing straight up instead of all hunched over and your jaw isn't achy from yawning every five minutes. What's going on here? You don't remember feeling this good since before you conceived.

Hmmm, you think back and realize that you've actually been sleeping pretty well at night. In fact, it's been several weeks since you've had to wake up in the middle of the night. Maybe even a month! Maybe even two! Now that you think about it, you can't even remember the last time you had to talk down a nightmare, deal with a growing pain, or wake up at five in the morning with a flashlight shining in your eye and a kid telling you, "It's waffle time!"

Yes, after all these years and all your hard work, you're finally the parent of a kid who consistently sleeps through the night! Getting to this point was harder to endure than any college thesis, demanding boss, or low-carb diet. But it's finally over. At long last you don't walk around in a fog all day. You don't fall asleep during sex. And you don't (dare I say it?) regret the fact that you had a kid because you miss your old life so darn much (there, I said it)!

Suddenly you have a whole new outlook on life! The sky looks bluer, your whites look whiter, and your husband doesn't bug the hell out of you whenever he makes that gross noise when he chews. Never again will you take for granted the joy of sleeping for eight continuous hours. No more waking up to panicked calls from your child or kicks from your husband telling you it's your turn to go in.

From here on out, you can handle anything your kid throws your way. Defiance! Misbehavior! Tantrums . . . okay, maybe not tantrums because those are just plain hell. Having a kid who's a good sleeper has been your biggest dream, next to the one about finally being able to fit in your wedding dress again. And, after all these turbulent years, it's finally here . . . the sleeping part anyway. The dress, we're all still hoping. As of today, you're officially the parent of a child who sleeps through the night! Congratulations, my friend! You certainly deserve it! From here on in, sleep well, and pleasant dreams!

appendix

resources

How to Give a Baby a Massage

Wait a half-hour after you feed your baby. Puking is not conducive to relaxation. Get your baby naked. If the room is cold, use a blanket to cover up the parts that aren't being massaged. Rub some lotion in your hands and warm them up. Massage your baby, starting at his head and working down to his toes, making eye contact whenever possible. Don't rub any harder than you would if you were rubbing your eyelids. For complete instructions including visuals, go to *www.make wayforbaby.com.*

How to Swaddle a Baby

To make life easy, you can simply buy a swaddle blanket that has Velcro strips sewn in at precise locations for easy swaddling. But in a pinch, you can use any old receiving blanket and do the following.

Lay down the blanket and fold down the top corner. Lay your baby on top of the blanket with her neck just at the fold. Hold one of her arms at her side and fold over that side of the blanket, tucking it underneath her other side (i.e., if you're holding down her right arm, take the right corner, fold it over her and tuck it under her left side). Fold the bottom corner up onto that same side. Now hold down her opposite arm, fold over that corner, and tuck it tightly under her other side. Don't be afraid to swaddle her good and tight . . . not so tight as to cut off circulation, but tight enough to make her feel snug as a bug in a rug, who's wearing a straightjacket.

How to Train Your Dog

If you have a dog that you think could be a problem once you bring home a baby, here are some good training books that could help stop annoying barking, jumping up, or any other behavior that may not mix with a newborn.

Don't Shoot the Dog! The New Art of Teaching and Training by Karen Pryor (Bantam)

The Other End of the Leash: Why We Do What We Do Around Dogs by Patricia B. McConnell, Ph.D. (Ballantine Books)

The Dog Whisperer: A Compassionate, Nonviolent Approach to Dog Training by Paul Owens with Norma Eckroate (Adams Media)

Cesar's Way: The Natural, Everyday Guide to Understanding & Correcting Common Dog Problems by Cesar Millan (Harmony)

(Note: No, I haven't read it, but the guy has his own show, and he's been on *Oprah* for heaven's sake. He must do something right.)

Marley & Me: Life and Love with the World's Worst Dog by John Grogan (William Morrow)

(Note: Okay, technically it's not a dog training book, but for a dog lover, it's a great read!)

Tracking Your Baby's Sleep Patterns

If you're interested in tracking your baby's sleeping habits, here's what you need to put on each
form. If you want to read more, pick up a copy of
The No-Cry Sleep Solution by Elizabeth Pantley.

The first log is a napping log that keeps track
of what time your kid fell asleep for his nap, how
long he slept, what he was doing when he fell
asleep (like was he in a bouncy chair or in the
car), where he slept (like on the sofa or in your
arms), and if he was doing anything before he
went down for the nap (like nursing or being
rocked when he fell asleep).

Next is the pre-bedtime routine log that
records what your baby was doing two hours
before bedtime. There should be a space for the
time your baby fell asleep, what activities she was
doing during those two hours, at what level the
activities were (from active to calm), how loud
they were (from loud to quiet), and what the
light was like (from bright to dark).

The third log is one that tracks your baby's
waking at night. In this log you should make
note of what time your kid woke up, how he woke
you (which, in most cases, means that he cried),
how long your kid stayed awake before nodding
off again, how you got your kid to finally nod

off, and how long your child slept since he last fell asleep. Then there should be a summary of the night's performance listing total asleep time, total awake time, total number of awakenings, the longest span of sleep time, and the total number of hours that he slept.

Wow! Looks as if you'll put in more hours than I did writing this whole book!

index

about the author

Joanne Kimes has written for several children's television shows, comedy shows, and numerous magazines, and is the author of eight books for the *Sucks* series including the bestselling *Pregnancy Sucks*. More importantly, after years of dealing with her daughter's sleeping issues, she now enjoys eight continuous hours of shut-eye each night! She lives with her husband and daughter in Studio City, CA.